Y0-ASM-446

The VOLUME 3 Digital Photography Book

The step-by-step secrets for how to
make your photos look like the pros'!

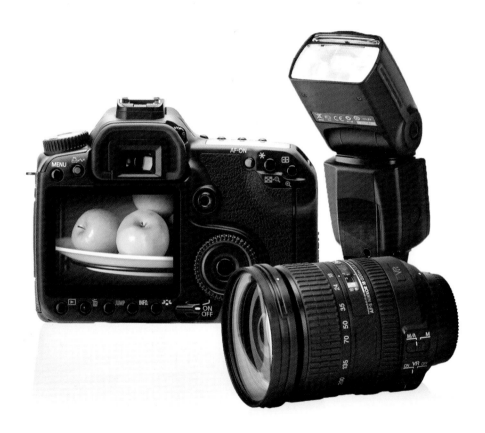

Scott Kelby

The Digital Photography Book, volume 3

The Digital Photography Book, volume 3 Team

TECHNICAL EDITORS
Kim Doty
Cindy Snyder

EDITORIAL CONSULTANT
Brad Moore

CREATIVE DIRECTOR
Felix Nelson

TRAFFIC DIRECTOR
Kim Gabriel

PRODUCTION MANAGER
Dave Damstra

GRAPHIC DESIGN
Jessica Maldonado

COVER DESIGNED BY
Jessica Maldonado

STUDIO AND
PRODUCTION SHOTS
Brad Moore
Rafael "RC" Concepcion

PUBLISHED BY
Peachpit Press

Copyright ©2010 by Scott Kelby

FIRST EDITION: July 2009

Composed in Myriad Pro (Adobe Systems Incorporated) and Lucida Grande (Bigelow & Holmes Inc.) by Kelby Media Group.

Trademarks
All terms mentioned in this book that are known to be trademarks or service marks have been appropriately capitalized. Peachpit Press cannot attest to the accuracy of this information. Use of a term in the book should not be regarded as affecting the validity of any trademark or service mark.

Photoshop, Elements, and Lightroom are registered trademarks of Adobe Systems Incorporated. Nikon is a registered trademark of Nikon Corporation. Canon is a registered trademark of Canon Inc.

Warning and Disclaimer
This book is designed to provide information about digital photography. Every effort has been made to make this book as complete and as accurate as possible, but no warranty of fitness is implied.

The information is provided on an as-is basis. The author and Peachpit Press shall have neither the liability nor responsibility to any person or entity with respect to any loss or damages arising from the information contained in this book or from the use of the discs or programs that may accompany it.

THIS PRODUCT IS NOT ENDORSED OR SPONSORED BY ADOBE SYSTEMS INCORPORATED, PUBLISHER OF ADOBE PHOTOSHOP, PHOTOSHOP ELEMENTS, AND PHOTOSHOP LIGHTROOM.

ISBN 10:   0-321-61765-7
ISBN 13: 978-0-321-61765-1

9 8

Printed and bound in the United States of America

www.kelbytraining.com
www.peachpit.com

For my in-house editor Kim Doty.
One of the best things that ever
happened to my books is you.

Acknowledgments

Although only one name appears on the spine of this book, it takes a team of dedicated and talented people to pull a project like this together. I'm not only delighted to be working with them, but I also get the honor and privilege of thanking them here.

To my amazing wife Kalebra: This year we're celebrating our 20th wedding anniversary, and I'm more in love, more crazy about you, and more thrilled that you're my wife than ever. Besides being a world-class mother, a gourmet chef, an artist, a singer, and a brilliant businesswoman, you're just about the coolest person I've ever known. I still can't believe that you chose me, and I'll spend the rest of my life working to make sure you always feel you made the right choice. I love you, sweetheart.

To my wonderful, crazy, fun-filled, little buddy Jordan: If there's any kid on the planet who knows how much their dad loves them, and how proud their dad is of them, it's you little buddy (even though, now that you're 12, I'm not supposed to call you "little buddy" anymore. Well, at least not in front of your friends). You were wired at the factory to be an incredibly fun, hilarious, creative, positive, sensitive, super-bright, yet totally crazy kid, and I love it. But I have to admit, as much fun as I have at our nightly *Halo 3* battles on Xbox LIVE, last week when I dragged my amp and guitar up to your room, you sat down at your drums, and we jammed on an extended version of Bon Jovi's "You Give Love a Bad Name," I knew at that moment that if it was possible to have become a luckier dad than I already was, it just happened. Dude (I mean, son), you rock!

To my beautiful "big girl" Kira: You're totally blessed with your mom's outer beauty, and also something that's even more important: her inner beauty, warmth, compassion, smarts, and charm, which will translate into the loving, fun- and adventure-filled, thrilling, drive-it-like-you-stole-it kind of life so many people dream of. You were born with a smile on your lips, a song in your heart, and a dad that is totally wrapped around your finger.

To my big brother Jeff: A lot of younger brothers look up to their older brothers because, well…they're older. But I look up to you because you've been much more than a brother to me. It's like you've been my "other dad" in the way you always looked out for me, gave me wise and thoughtful council, and always put me first—just like Dad put us first. Your boundless generosity, kindness, positive attitude, and humility have been an inspiration to me my entire life, and I'm just so honored to be your brother and lifelong friend.

To my best buddy Dave Moser: Do you know how great it is to get to work every day with your best buddy? I do. It's awesome. Thanks my friend—you are the best.

To my in-house team at Kelby Media Group: I am incredibly blessed to go to work each day with a group of uniquely dedicated, self-motivated, and incredibly creative people—people who mean much more to me than just employees, and everything they do says they feel the same way. My humble thanks to you all for allowing me to work with the very best every day.

To my editor Kim Doty: What can I say—this book is dedicated to you! Writing books is never easy, but you make my job so much easier by keeping me on track and organized, and for staying absolutely calm and positive in the face of every storm. One of the luckiest things that has ever happened to my books is that you came along to edit them, and I'm very honored and grateful to have you making my books so much better than what I turned in.

To Jessica Maldonado: You are, hands-down, the Diva of Design, and I owe much of the success of my books to the wonderful look and feel you give them. What you do brings my books to life, and helps them reach a wider audience than they ever would have, and I'm so thrilled that you're the person that works these miracles for us (signed, your biggest fan!).

To Cindy Snyder: A big, big thanks for helping tech and copyedit all the tips in the book and, as always, for catching lots of little things that others would have missed.

To Dave Damstra: You give my books such a spot-on, clean, to-the-point look, and although I don't know how you do it, I sure am glad that you do!

To my friend and longtime Creative Director Felix Nelson: We love you. We all do. We always have. We always will. You're Felix. There's only one.

To my Executive Assistant and general Wonder Woman Kathy Siler: You are one of the most important people in the building, not only for all the wonderful things you do for me, but for all the things you do for our entire business. Thanks for always looking out for me, for keeping me focused, and for making sure I have the time I need to write books, do seminars, and still have time with my family. You don't have an easy job, but you make it look easy.

To my photography assistant and digital tech Brad Moore: I don't know how I would have gotten through this book without your help, your work in the studio (shooting so many of the product shots), your advice and input, and your patience. You've only been here a short time and you're already having a big impact. I'm so grateful to have someone of your talent and character on our team.

To my buddy RC Concepcion: My personal thanks for reprising your gig from volume 2, and stepping in to help get the studio shots done for this volume. You are the Swiss Army knife of digital imaging and design.

To Kim Gabriel: You continue to be the unsung hero behind the scenes, and I'm sure I don't say this enough, but thank you so much for everything you do to make this all come together.

To my dear friend and business partner Jean A. Kendra: Thanks for putting up with me all these years, and for your support for all my crazy ideas. It really means a lot.

To my editor at Peachpit Press, Ted Waitt: Do you know what a joy it is to work on a photo book with an editor who's also a passionate and creative photographer? It makes a huge difference. You get it. You get me. I get you. It's a beautiful thing.

To my publisher Nancy Aldrich-Ruenzel, Scott Cowlin, Sarah Jane Todd, and the incredibly dedicated team at Peachpit Press: It's a real honor to get to work with people who really just want to make great books.

To all the talented and gifted photographers who've taught me so much over the years: Moose Peterson, Vincent Versace, Bill Fortney, David Ziser, Jim DiVitale, Helene Glassman, Joe McNally, Anne Cahill, George Lepp, Kevin Ames, Eddie Tapp, and Jay Maisel, my sincere and heartfelt thanks for sharing your passion, ideas, and techniques with me and my students.

To my mentors John Graden, Jack Lee, Dave Gales, Judy Farmer, and Douglas Poole: Your wisdom and whip-cracking have helped me immeasurably throughout my life, and I will always be in your debt, and grateful for your friendship and guidance.

Most importantly, I want to thank God, and His son Jesus Christ, for leading me to the woman of my dreams, for blessing us with such amazing children, for allowing me to make a living doing something I truly love, for always being there when I need Him, for blessing me with a wonderful, fulfilling, and happy life, and such a warm, loving family to share it with.

Other Books By Scott Kelby

Scott Kelby's 7-Point System for Adobe Photoshop CS3

The Digital Photography Book, vols. 1 & 2

The Photoshop Elements Book for Digital Photographers

The Adobe Photoshop Lightroom Book for Digital Photographers

The Photoshop Book for Digital Photographers

The Photoshop Channels Book

Photoshop Down & Dirty Tricks

Photoshop Killer Tips

Photoshop Classic Effects

The iPod Book

InDesign Killer Tips

Mac OS X Leopard Killer Tips

The iPhone Book

About the Author

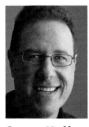

Scott Kelby

Scott is Editor, Publisher, and co-founder of *Photoshop User* magazine, Editor-in-Chief of *Layers* magazine (the how-to magazine for everything Adobe), and is the co-host of the weekly video podcasts *DTown TV* (the weekly show for Nikon dSLR shooters) and *Photoshop User TV*.

He is President of the National Association of Photoshop Professionals (NAPP), the trade association for Adobe® Photoshop® users, and he's President of the software training, education, and publishing firm Kelby Media Group.

Scott is a photographer, designer, and award-winning author of more than 50 books, including *The Digital Photography Book*, volumes 1 and 2, *The Adobe Photoshop Book for Digital Photographers*, *Photoshop Down & Dirty Tricks*, *The Adobe Photoshop Lightroom Book for Digital Photographers*, *Photoshop Classic Effects*, *The iPod Book*, and *The iPhone Book*.

For five years straight, Scott has been honored with the distinction of being the world's #1 best-selling author of all computer and technology books, across all categories. His books have been translated into dozens of different languages, including Chinese, Russian, Spanish, Korean, Polish, Taiwanese, French, German, Italian, Japanese, Dutch, Swedish, Turkish, and Portuguese, among others, and he is a recipient of the prestigious Benjamin Franklin Award.

Scott is Training Director for the Adobe Photoshop Seminar Tour, and Conference Technical Chair for the Photoshop World Conference & Expo. He's featured in a series of training DVDs and online courses, and has been training photographers and Adobe Photoshop users since 1993.

For more information on Scott and his photography, visit his daily blog at www.scottkelby.com

Table of Contents

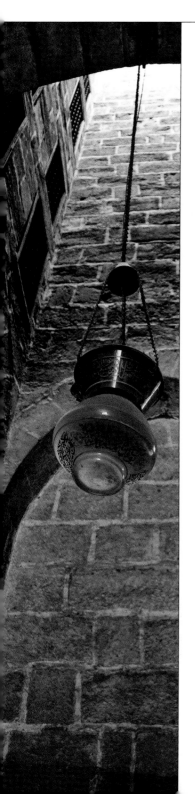

Table of Contents

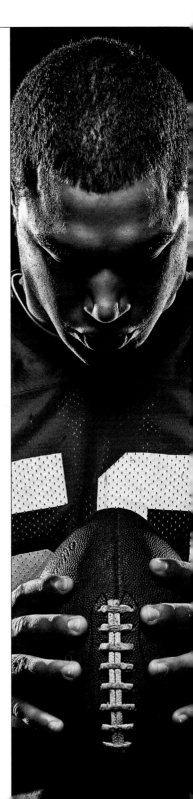

Table of Contents

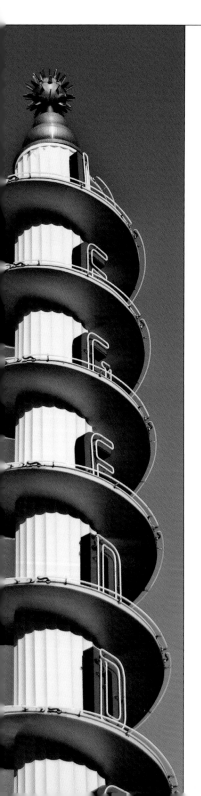

Table of Contents

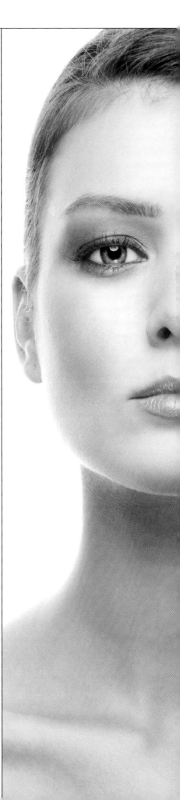

Table of Contents

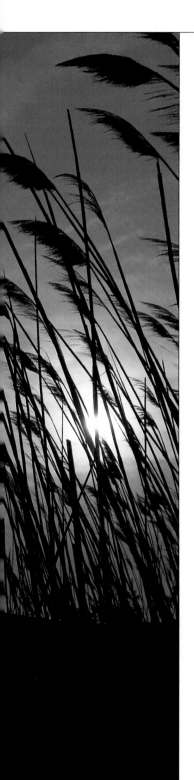

Table of Contents

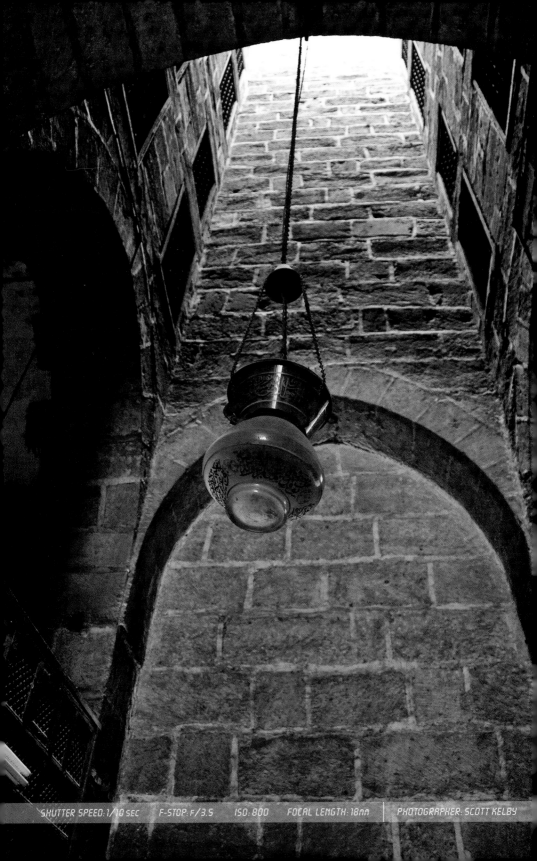

Chapter One

Using Flash Like a Pro, Part 2

Picking Right Up Where the Last Book Left Off

I know what you're thinking: "If this is Part 2, where is Part 1?" Well, Part 1 is actually Chapter One back in volume 2. "Wait a darn minute—you're pulling that old 'bait and switch' scam, right?" No, a bait-and-switch scam is where you see an advertisement for a washer and dryer for a really low price (the bait), but then you go to the store and they tell you it's sold out, and then they try to talk you into buying a more expensive washer and dryer that they have in stock (that's the switch). My scam is totally different: (1) This book isn't about washers or dryers, and (2) I didn't offer a cheaper book, and then try to trick you into buying a more expensive book. Instead, my scam is called a "jump back," where I'm trying to get you to buy more books. Here's how it works: You've already bought volume 3 (the book you're holding in your hands right now), but on the first page of the book (this page), you realize that you should have bought volume 2 first, because it had a chapter with the most essential stuff about wireless flash. That way, you'd be ready for the stuff in this chapter, which is what people who read volume 2 told me they wanted to learn about next. So now, you have to "jump back" in your car (get it?) and head to the bookstore to buy volume 2. But, then, once you're home and you start reading volume 2, you soon realize that I assume if you're reading volume 2 that you have already read volume 1, so I skip over stuff that I figure you already learned in volume 1. Now you have to "jump back" in the car again and go buy volume 1, as well. It's a classic jump-back scam, but of course I would never admit that, especially here in the book. The whole thing is like the hit TV show *Lost*. If you didn't start watching it until Season 3, you'd realize it was aptly named.

9 Things You'll Wish You Had Known...

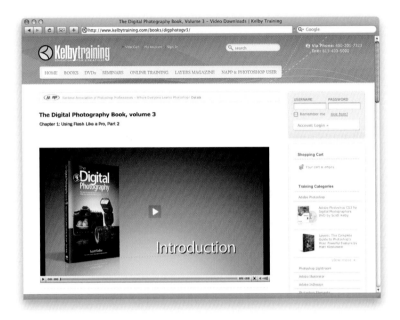

(1) **You don't have to read this part.** That's because I created a video that explains how to get the most out of this book. It's really short and to the point, but I promise you it will make using and learning from this book much more enjoyable (plus, then you can skip reading this section, because the video covers it all). You can find the video at **www.kelbytraining.com/books/digphotogv3**.

(2) **Here's how this book works:** Basically, it's you and me together at a shoot, and I'm giving you the same tips, the same advice, and sharing the same techniques I've learned over the years from some of the top working pros. But when I'm with a friend, I skip all the technical stuff. So, for example, if you turned to me and said, "Hey Scott, I want the light to look really soft and flattering. How far back should I put this softbox?" I wouldn't give you a lecture about lighting ratios or flash modifiers. In real life, I'd just turn to you and say, "Move it in as close as you can to your subject, without it actually showing up in the shot. The closer you get, the softer and more wrapping the light gets." I'd tell you short, and right to the point. Like that. So that's what I do here.

(3) **This picks up right where volume 2 left off,** and this stuff in this book is what people who bought volume 2 told me they wanted to learn next. So, for example, in the chapter on wireless flash, I don't show you how to set up your flash to be wireless, because all that type of stuff was already covered in the flash chapter in volume 2. Instead, it picks up right after that, with all new stuff. Now, should you have volumes 1 and 2 before…

...Before Reading This Book!

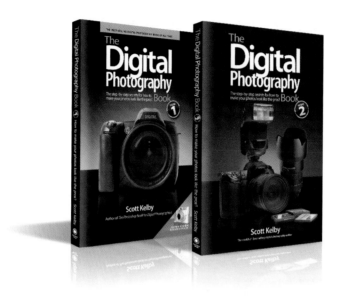

...you read this book? It's not absolutely necessary, but it certainly wouldn't bother me one bit if you did (like how I phrased that? A very subtle, soft-sell approach. Compelling, but yet not overbearing). All joking aside, if you're into off-camera flash or studio lighting, it is helpful to have read at least volume 2, because those chapters in this book figure you already learned the basics in volume 2.

(4) Sometimes you have to buy stuff. This is not a book to sell you stuff, but before you move forward, understand that to get pro results, sometimes you have to use some accessories that the pros use. I don't get a kickback or promo fee from any companies whose products I recommend. I'm just giving you the exact same advice I'd give a friend.

(5) Where do I find all this stuff? Since I didn't want to fill the book with a bunch of Web links (especially since webpages can change without notice), I put together a special page for you at my site with a link to any of the gear I mention here in the book. You can find this gear page at **www.kelbytraining.com/books/vol3gear**.

(6) The intro page at the beginning of each chapter is just designed to give you a quick mental break, and honestly, they have little to do with the chapter. In fact, they have little to do with anything, but writing these off-the-wall chapter intros is kind of a tradition of mine (I do this in all my books), so if you're one of those really "serious" types, please, I'm begging you—skip them, because they'll just get on your nerves.

That Was Only 6. Here Are the Last 3

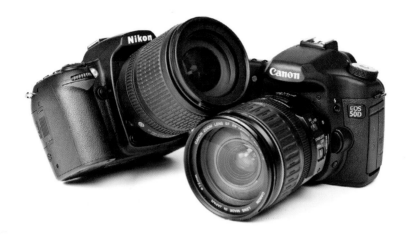

(7) If you're shooting with a Sony or Olympus or a Sigma digital camera, don't let it throw you that a Nikon or Canon camera is pictured. Since most people are shooting with a Nikon or Canon, I usually show one or the other, but don't sweat it if you're not—most of the techniques in this book apply to any digital SLR camera, and many of the point-and-shoot digital cameras, as well.

(8) **There are extra tips at the bottom of a lot of pages**—sometimes they relate to the technique on that particular page, and sometimes I just had a tip and needed to fit it somewhere, so I put it on that page. So, you should probably at least take a quick glance anytime you see a tip box on the bottom of a page—ya know, just in case.

(9) **Keep this in mind: This is a "show me how to do it" book.** I'm telling you these tips just like I'd tell a shooting buddy, and that means oftentimes it's just which button to push, which setting to change, where to put the light, and not a whole lot of reasons why. I figure that once you start getting amazing results from your camera, you'll go out and buy one of those "tell me all about it" digital camera or lighting books. I do truly hope this book ignites your passion for photography by helping you get the kind of results you always hoped you'd get from your digital photography. Now, pack up your gear, it's time to head out for our first shoot.

Soft Light on Location (the Budget Way)

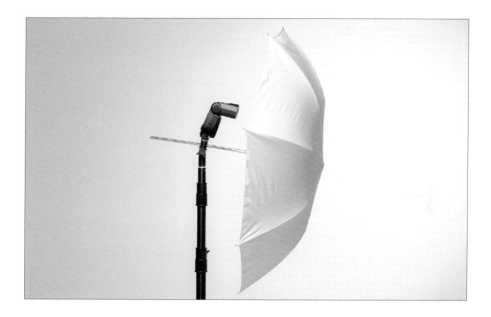

Back in *The Digital Photography Book*, volume 2, I went into great detail about how important it is to diffuse and soften the light from your small flash, so you get professional looking
results. Although I usually have you firing through diffusers, here's another way to get the
job done, which is particularly handy for people shooting without an assistant or anyone
who can help wrangle the gear during the shoot: use a shoot-through umbrella setup. Now,
before I get into this, I want to say up front that I just flat-out don't like reflective umbrellas,
where you aim the umbrella and flash away from your subject, then the light from your flash
hits the inside of the umbrella and travels back toward your subject like a lighting grenade.
Yeech! However, in this case, you're actually aiming the flash at your subject, and you're using
a special translucent shoot-through umbrella that's designed to let you fire your small flash
directly through it and right at your subject, giving you a much more concentrated beam
than a reflective umbrella does. The advantages are: (1) you can get softer wraparound light
with it because you can put the umbrella very close to your subject, (2) it's an umbrella, so it's
very compact, (3) you can control how large your light source actually is (see the next page),
and (4) it's incredibly inexpensive for a pro setup (yes, a lot of working pros use a similar
setup). To make this all work, you need three things (besides your flash unit, of course): a
shoot-through umbrella (I use a Westcott 43" Optical White Satin Collapsible shoot-through
umbrella, which sells for around $20); a tilting umbrella bracket, with a flash shoe to support
the flash and a slot for the umbrella to slide through (I use a LumoPro LP633 Umbrella Swivel
with Flash Shoe Adapter which sells for around $18); and a lightweight light stand (I use a
Manfrotto lightweight 6'2" Nano Stand—around $60). So, the whole setup is just under $100.

Controlling Softness with an Umbrella

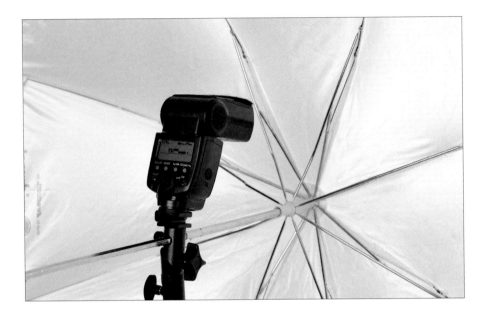

If you're using a shoot-through umbrella, you have to decide how soft you want the light to be that comes through that umbrella. Well, this is partially controlled by how far back you place the flash from the inside of the umbrella. I usually want really soft light for shooting things like brides, and portraits of families, etc., so I slide the umbrella out around two feet from the flash. That way, the light from the flash fills as much of the umbrella as possible, making my light source bigger, which makes my light softer (remember that from volume 2? The bigger the light source, the softer the light?). If you want sharper, edgier light, you know what to do—slide the umbrella in the adapter, so it's much closer to the flash. Now the flash has much less room to spread, and your light will be smaller, more direct, and less soft.

Get More Control Using a Portable Softbox

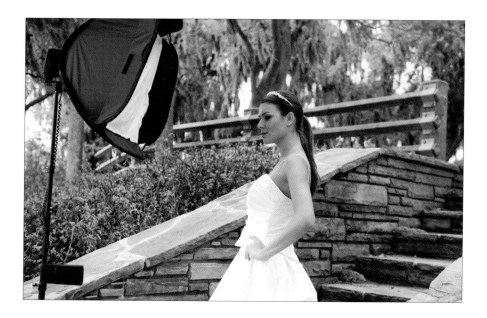

If you've got a few more bucks to spend, then you can move up to a small softbox designed for off-camera flash. I think there are two big advantages to using this over a shoot-through umbrella: (1) The light is more contained and directional than with a shoot-through umbrella, so it's easier to get more dramatic light, since it only goes where you aim it. (2) They don't seem to blow over as easy when using them outdoors. This is bigger than it sounds, because umbrellas catch the wind like you can't believe, and even the slightest wind can send the whole thing (umbrella, stand, and your flash) crashing over. The small-flash softbox I use is the Lastolite Ezybox. I like that it's so small and portable—it collapses down to a small round shape (like a reflector)—and it sets up without having to use steel rods, so it only takes two minutes. Plus, I love the quality of its soft, directional light. There are different sizes, but I use the 24x24" size.

Hand-Holding an Ezybox

You don't have to use a light stand to hold your flash and Ezybox. You can have a friend (or a bridesmaid, or an assistant, etc.) hold them using a special accessory, which is a small (24" tall), lightweight, hand-held stand with a handle on the bottom that lets your Ezybox pretty much go anywhere your friend can go, turning your friend into what has become known in flash circles as a VAL (the acronym for a voice-activated light stand).

What Your Flash's Groups Are For

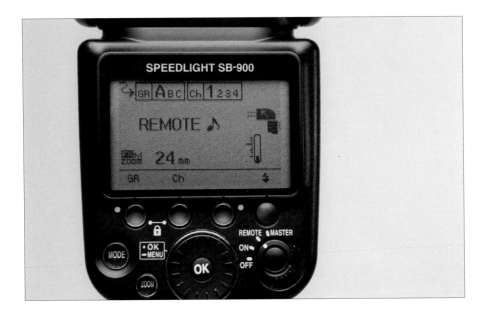

If you want to control your wireless flashes independently of each other, then you need groups. For example, let's say that you have one flash off to the left of your subject, and one flash behind the subject lighting a white seamless background. You'd want to be able to control the power of each flash individually, so if the background flash is too bright, you can turn it down without having the front flash power down, as well. You do that by assigning one flash to Group A, then the other flash (the background flash) to Group B. Now you can control the power of each one individually, without disturbing the other. Also, you can have more than one flash in each group. So, if you have two flashes on the background (one lighting the left side; one lighting the right), and you put them both on Group B, they would move up/down in power together, but your front flash (which is still on Group A) would be unaffected. Sweet! You assign a flash to a particular group right on the flash unit itself.

What Your Flash's Channels Are For

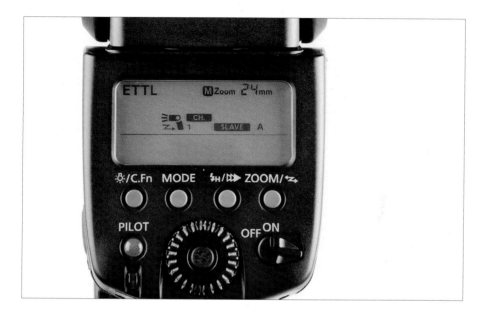

As long as you're by yourself, just you and your flash, things are good. But what happens if you're hired to shoot an event, like a wedding for example, and you have a second (or third) photographer shooting along with you (it's more and more common to have a second shooter at a wedding—especially weddings in Texas, where the ceremony is held on a grassy knoll. Sorry, that was lame)? The problem you'd probably face is that sometimes the second shooter's camera would trigger and fire your flash (and vice versa). That's why your flash has different channels. At the beginning of the wedding, you'd set your flash to Channel 1, and you'd tell your second shooter to set their flash to Channel 2. That way, your camera will only trigger your flash, and theirs will only trigger their flash. By the way, you have to set the channel in two places: (1) on the wireless flash unit itself, and (2) on whatever you're using to trigger your flash. For example, if you're shooting Nikon and the second shooter is using their camera's built-in Commander unit to control their wireless flash, you'd need to have them set their Commander to Channel 2. If you're shooting Canon, then you're probably using another flash mounted on your camera's hot shoe as your master flash, and in that case, you'd set that flash to Channel 2. If all of this "master" and "wireless" stuff sounds confusing, then you now know why I said you really need to read volume 2 of this book first, because it covers all the basics of wireless flash. Then all this would make more sense (and it would sell another book, which isn't a bad thing).

Using a Transmitter to Fire Your Flash

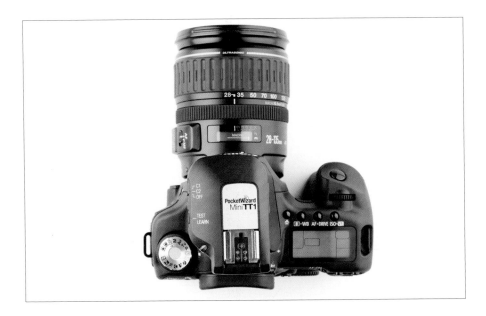

Back in volume 2 of this book, I showed you how to set up your small hot-shoe flash, so that your off-camera flash can be wireless, which is very cool (and makes your flash really usable). But there is a downside to using the built-in wireless system, and that is that the flashes have to be in the line of sight of whichever flash is your master flash (so, for example, if you're triggering your wireless flashes using the pop-up flash from your camera, the light sensor on the side of each of the wireless flashes has to be in the line of sight of the master flash [the pop-up flash], so they can sense the little light-pulse it emits as a signal for wireless flashes to fire. If they can't clearly see that light pulse, they won't fire). That's why many working pros use a dedicated wireless transmitter and receiver for firing their flashes—that way, the flashes fire 100% of the time, whether they can see the flash on your camera or not, because now the wireless transmitter is doing the firing for you. PocketWizard (longtime maker of wireless gear for studio work) has come up with a special wireless system for small off-camera flash called the MiniTT1™ Radio Slave Transmitter, which fits right on your camera's hot shoe, and then your master flash goes on top of that. Of course, the downside to this is you need to buy a transmitter unit, and then a receiver unit for each flash, but then your flash-firing troubles simply go away.

How to See If All Your Flashes Will Really Fire

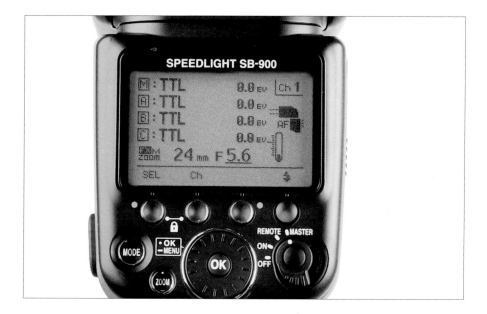

Let's say you've got four different flashes, and each one is assigned to a different group (just for the sake of this example, let's say we're shooting a studio portrait, and the main flash up front is on Group A, a hair light is assigned to Group B, and two background flashes are assigned to Group C). How can you tell if they're all going to fire? You can run a test! Just press the red test firing button on the back of your master flash unit, and each group will fire its flashes, in order, one after another, so you can see that they all work. (Note: It fires Group A's flashes first, then Group B's, and then the two background flashes on Group C last.) You'll visually see each one flash. If one doesn't fire, then you'll need to do some troubleshooting (make sure the non-firing flash is actually turned on, make sure it's assigned to the right group, make sure its sensor is seeing the flash from the master flash, etc.).

Shorten the Time Between Flashes

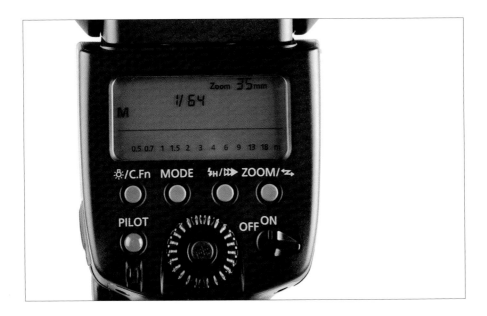

Each time your flash fires, since it's battery powered, it has to recycle before you can fire it again. When you first pop a fresh set of batteries into your flash, the recycle time is about as fast as it's going to get—probably just a few seconds between flashes. However, the more times your flash fires, the more your batteries wear down, and pretty soon a few seconds between flashes turns into five seconds, then 10 seconds, then 12 seconds, and then it just feels like an eternity, and you know it's time to change batteries. However, there's another way to shorten the recycle time, and that is to lower the power of your flash. That's right—the lower the power, the faster the flash will recycle. Of course, lowering the power of your flash will make your subject look darker, because now there's less light from your flash falling on your subject, so you'll have to adjust your f-stop so your image looks good. For example, if you're shooting at 1/64 power at f/5.6, you'll need to change your f-stop to at least f/4, if not f/2.8, to brighten the overall exposure, and make your flash balance out again.

Recycle Faster with an External Battery Pack

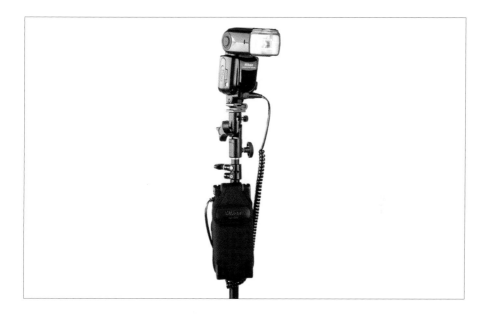

If you're doing some serious location flash work (like a wedding, on-location fashion shoot, etc.), or anything where you need the shortest possible recycle time with the longest battery life, then try using an external battery pack, like Nikon's SD-9 for the SB-900 (which holds eight AA batteries), or Canon's Compact Battery Pack CP-E4 (which also holds eight AA batteries). What these do is reassign how the batteries inside your flash work. Usually, those four batteries inside run both the recycling and all the software requirements of the flash unit. When you attach one of these external battery packs, it assigns all the recycling duties to those eight AA batteries, so you get longer battery life and much faster recycling times. Use one of these once, and you'll never be without one again.

Another Recycle–Faster Tip

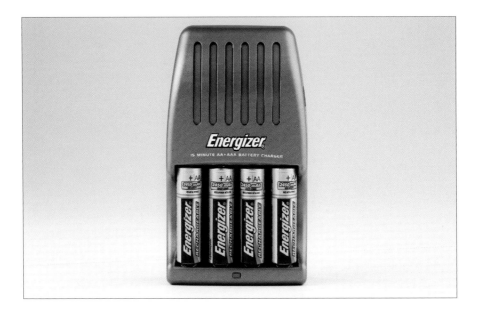

If you use off-camera flash a lot, you're going to be going through a lot of batteries, and you'll probably want to get rechargeable ones, so you don't go broke buying batteries all the time. But beyond that, there's another advantage to using rechargeable batteries (which I learned from David Hobby of Strobist.com fame), as long as you buy nickel-metal hydride (NiMH) batteries. Because of their lower voltage, they recycle much faster (in flashes, anyway) than regular alkaline AA batteries. Plus, you can recharge a set of four in about 15 minutes (in fact, Energizer sells what they call their 15-Minute Charger for nickel-metal hydride batteries). I would buy two sets of AA nickel-metal hydrides—one set in the flash, and another set as your backup on location. If you need to switch to the backup set, you could always throw the first set in the charger, so they'll be ready if you need 'em again (and if that's the case, you're really poppin' a lot of flashes!).

Charge 'em Right Before You Use 'em

Nickel-metal hydride batteries discharge around 10% of their battery life per week if they're just sitting around doing nothing, so don't charge up your batteries until you need 'em for a job—that way they'll be at full capacity.

Typical Power Settings for Your Flash

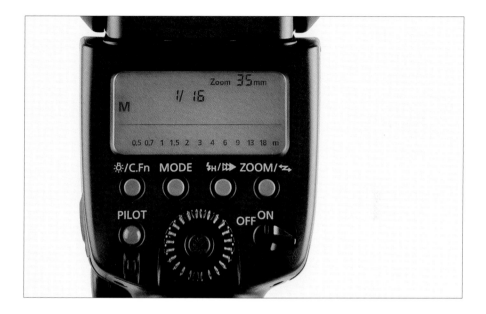

If you're using your flash indoors, or outdoors in anything other than bright daylight, you'll be running your flash 99% of the time at less than half-power. In fact, you'll prob-ably be often running it at 25% power (I'm sometimes at 1/8 or 1/16 power during a typical shoot). Why so low? Because the idea is to balance the light from your flash with the existing light already in the room (or already available outside), so you usually want just a little bit of flash (or your flash will look like flash). The goal is to make your flash look like natural light, so your power setting will probably stay real darn low.

Firing a Second Flash in Another Room

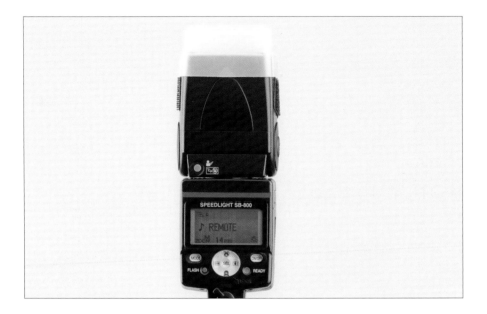

Let's say you're shooting the interior of a home and lighting it with off-camera flash. Nothing looks worse than seeing an adjoining room (maybe the dining room in the background) looking all dark, so you put a second flash in there and aim it at the ceiling to light that room. So far so good. Now, of course, in that dining room you don't want to actually see the flash unit itself, so you hide it from view, right? Here comes the problem: these flashes work on "line of sight" (meaning your second flash has to have an unobstructed view of the master flash. If it doesn't, it won't fire). So, here's the trick to get around that: you set your flash to Remote (or Slave) mode (depending of which brand of flash you own), and then it doesn't have to be in the line of sight anymore—if it detects even a tiny hint of light from the flash in the main room, that puppy fires! Keep this in mind the next time you need to hide a second flash, or put it where the whole line-of-sight thing won't work.

Overpowering the Sun

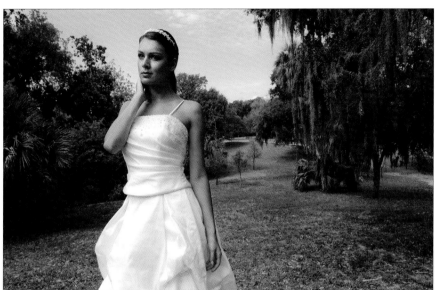

SCOTT KELBY

This technique is very popular with wedding photographers who shoot outdoors. It uses your flash on your subject, who is in broad daylight. They call this "overpowering the sun," but what you're really going to do is set your exposure for a regular daylight shot, then intentionally underexpose the shot by a stop or two, so the photo looks a little dark. Then, you'll turn on your flash, and let it light your subject instead of the sun, which produces a very commercial look. So, first switch your camera to program mode, then hold the shutter button halfway down and look at the settings your camera chose to properly expose this daylight shot. Let's say it's 1/80 of a second at f/11. Switch to manual mode, and dial in 1/80 of a second at f/11. Now, to make the scene darker (underexposed), you'd just change the f-stop to f/16. Take a test shot and see if it's dark enough. If not, drop it down to f/22 and make another test shot. Once it's obviously underexposed, now you turn on your flash, and use it to light your subject. Outdoors, I usually start at full power, and if it looks too bright, I try lowering the power of my flash a bit and then take another test shot. Keep lowering the flash power until the image looks balanced (like the shot above, taken in the middle of the afternoon in direct sunlight).

Getting the Ring Flash Look Using Small Flash

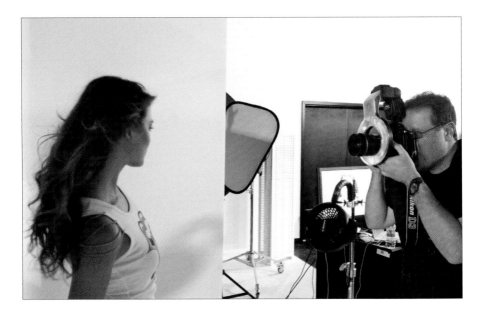

It's one of those looks you either love or you just can't stand (with its flat, bright look and hard-edged shadow behind the subject), and you're probably better off if you don't like it, because ring flashes are big, bulky, and fairly expensive. However, there is a ring flash adapter that fits over your off-camera flash that does a surprisingly good job of giving you the ring flash look (which has become incredibly popular in high-end fashion photography these days) without the ring flash price, weight, or size. It's called the Ray Flash—it slides right over your flash head, and your lens extends through the center of the flash (as seen above). It basically redirects the light from your existing flash into a ring shape and it's really lightweight and doesn't require batteries or anything else.

If You Long for a Real Ring Flash...

I did find a reasonably priced real ring flash from AlienBees that attaches to your camera, and while it is bulkier, heavier, and more expensive than the Ray Flash ring flash adapter shown above, it's not as bulky, heavy, or expensive as any of the other real ring flashes I've seen. I cover it on page 47 in Chapter 2.

What If Your Flash at Full Power Isn't Enough?

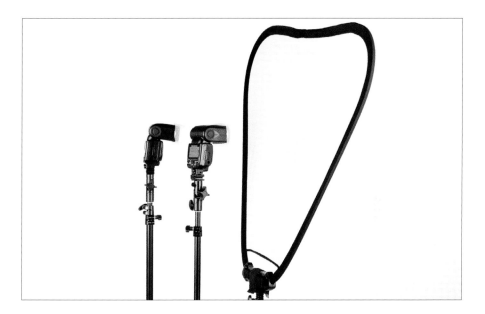

If you're lighting your subject, and your flash is at full power, but it's just not bright enough to do what you want it to do, just add another flash. That's right—pop another flash up there, right beside your other flash, but just make sure you put them both on the same group (so they'd both be assigned to Group A, or both assigned to Group B), so they both fire at the same time. Just like turning on another light in your home adds more light, adding another flash adds more light, too! By the way, adding another flash doesn't double your light output, it just adds about an extra stop of light. To add another stop of light, just add another two flashes, and so on.

Lowering the Power of Your Pop-Up Flash

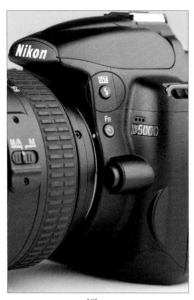

Nikon

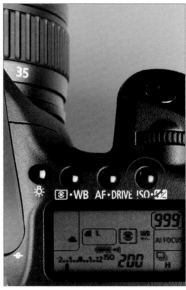

Canon

Some photographers use their camera's built-in pop-up flash as a fill flash when they're not trying to fully light the person they're shooting with flash, and they just want a little bit of flash to help fill in the shadows. The problem is your camera doesn't always know that you only want a little fill, and it usually sends more flash than you actually want, and the photo looks, well…it looks like you used a pop-up flash. However, most cameras actually have a setting that lets you lower the power of your pop-up flash, so if you try the ol' fill flash route and find that it looks more like regular flash, you can dial down the power of your pop-up and try again. On Nikon cameras, you do this by holding down the flash mode button (the one on the front side of your camera, right by the lens—it has a lightning bolt on it), then looking at the control panel on top, and turning the sub-command dial in front so you see a negative number. On Canon cameras, you press the ISO/flash exposure compensation button, look at the top LCD or viewfinder, and turn the quick control dial until you see a negative number. Then take a test shot, look at the results, and see if you need to lower the power some more.

When Not to Use a Diffusion Dome

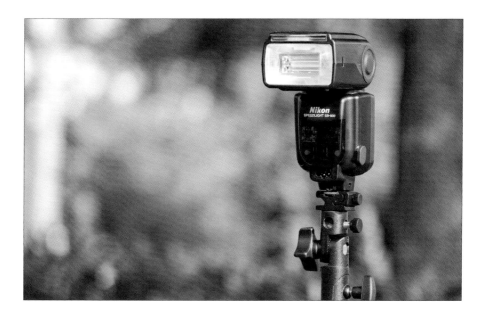

I leave my diffusion dome on my flash almost all the time (I'm usually looking to spread the light and make it softer), but there are a few instances where you don't want that dome on, and it's not just when you want hard, edgy light. For example, if your flash is far away from your subject, take the dome off, because when you're back that far, it will drain your batteries much faster, and since the light is far back, it's going to spread and soften a bit anyway. Another time you'd want to remove the dome is when you're outdoors using it as fill flash.

The Pro Trick for Better-Looking People Shots

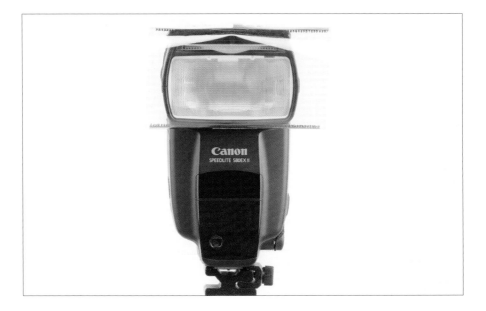

One inside tip a lot of big pros use when they're shooting portraits with small off-camera flash is to put a very light orange gel over the flash. It doesn't matter what time of day it is, that orange gel is over the front of their flash. The type of gel is called a ¼-cut of CTO (Color Temperature Orange). If you shoot people, I'd keep this on there all the time for better, more natural-looking color from your flash shots.

Two Other Gels You Really Need

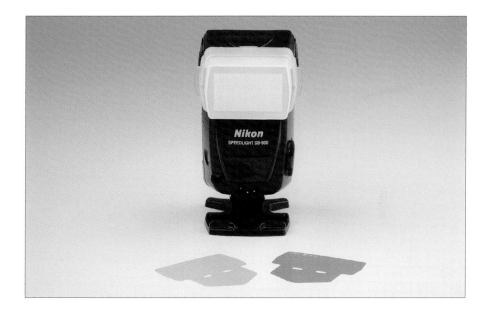

If you want natural-looking color from your flash (in other words, you want the light from your flash to blend in with the light already in the room), there are two colors of gels you're going to need to keep with you, which you put over your flash head: (1) an orange gel, for when you're shooting indoors under regular lighting (usually incandescent lighting), and (2) a green gel, for when you're shooting in an office or building under fluorescent lights.

You May Not Have to Buy These Gels

If you bought a Nikon SB-800, or the SB-900, both come with a set of gels (including the orange and green) right in the box.

Sticky Filters

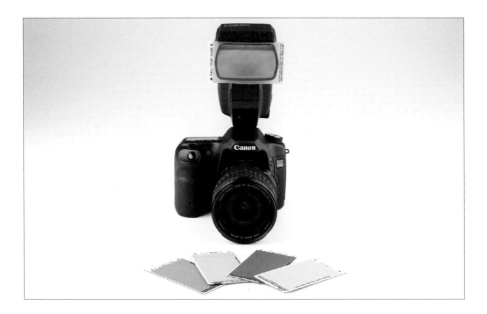

Gels, for some reason, seem to freak people out who are new to off-camera flash, and even mentioning gels in a live session brings up a host of questions like, "Where do I get them? How do I know if I'm getting the right ones? What colors should I get? How and where do I attach them to my flash? Do I need to cut them down to size?" Well, I guess a company named Midsouth Photographic Specialties heard this so many times, they finally went out and created a set of gels for off-camera flashes in the most requested colors, pre-cut to size, and ready to go. They're called Sticky Filters—just slap 'em on and you're set!

Tips for Lighting Your Background with Flash

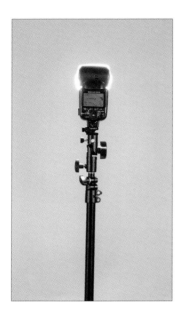 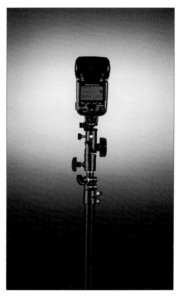

Here's a simple little rule that will help you when using your small off-camera flash to light a background wall or seamless background behind your subject. If you want to light the entire background fairly evenly, put your diffusion dome cap on the flash. This spreads the light out wide, and makes it appear smoother and more even (as shown here on the left). Then, back the flash itself away from the wall—the farther it is away, the more the light will spread. If, instead, you want a more defined "spotlight" look behind your subject, just move the flash in closer to the wall behind them and remove the diffusion dome (as shown here on the right).

Using That Little Flash Stand in the Box

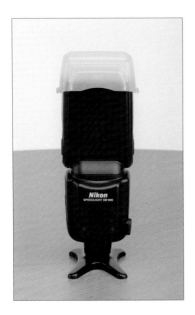
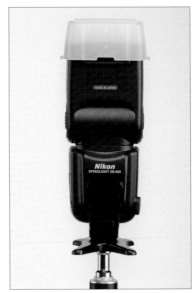

If you buy a Nikon or Canon flash, take a look inside the box it came in and you'll find a little black plastic stand (I call it a "foot," but Nikon calls it a "Speedlight stand" and Canon calls theirs a "mini stand"). Anyway, your flash slides right into this little stand, and now you can put your flash on the floor behind your subject, or on a table, and it stands right up. It's like a free mini-light-stand. However, it has a feature a lot of folks miss: the bottom is threaded, so you can screw it directly onto either a tripod, or a standard light stand, and it will hold your flash up higher. Hey, it saves you from having to buy a special adapter just to hold up your flash (though if you mount your flash on a stand a lot, and need a little more control [like tilt], then I'd use my tip from back in volume 2 and buy a Manfrotto Justin Spring Clamp with Flash Shoe for around $57, and then you can mount a flash just about anywhere).

Where You Focus Affects Your Flash Exposure

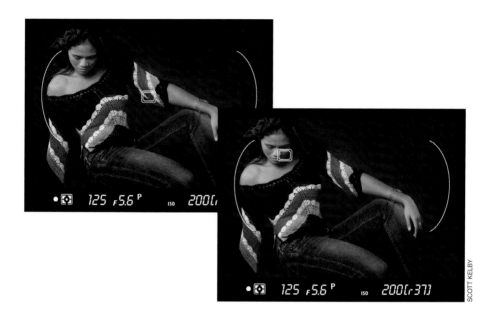

Today's small off-camera flashes do such a great job, partially because they adjust their power output based on the exposure for the shot (Canon calls this TTL for through-the-lens metering and Nikon calls this i-TTL for intelligent-through-the-lens metering, but they mean the same thing). So, why do you care? Well, your flash is going to help make the exposure based on exactly what you focus on in the photo. So, if you focus on your subject, it's going to try to give you a proper exposure for your subject, and vary the amount of flash power based on making your subject look good. However, if you focus on something else, like the background behind your subject, your flash is going to try to light that area instead. This is why, when using small off-camera flash, you need to make sure you're careful about focusing on the area you want to look best. If you do, your flash results will look that much better.

The Paid-Gig Flash Insurance Policy

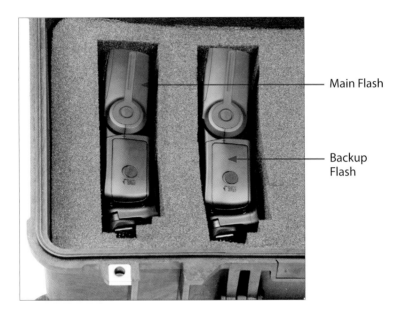

Main Flash

Backup
Flash

If you're hired to do a paid gig (like a wedding, or a portrait session, etc.), you want to make darn sure you have a backup flash, because if, for whatever reason, your first flash dies (you drop it, the wind knocks your flash over and it dies, there's some weird problem with the flash unit itself, etc.), at least you can grab the backup. That's not the tip, though. Having a backup for a paying job is an absolute necessity. Here's the tip: make sure the flash you use as a backup is the same make and model as your main flash. That way, if you suddenly have to switch flashes in the middle of the shoot, you're not trying to figure out how it works, or what the settings should be for a flash that doesn't have the same power output, or anything else that might freak you out (in front of the client), because you're not used to working with that model of flash. If you use the same make and model as your backup, and then you swap out flashes, it's just business as usual.

How High to Position Your Flash

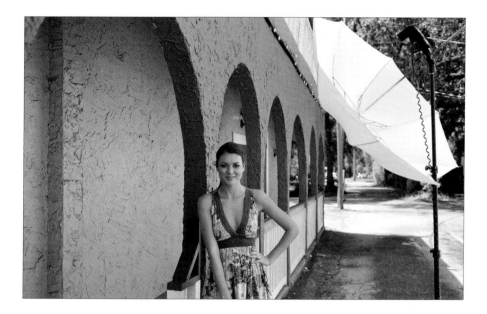

So, you've got your wireless flash all set up, your flash is on a light stand (or a friend is holding the flash for you), and now you're wondering, "How high up do I put this thing and where do I aim it?" Here's a simple way to think about it: position the flash where the sun would be. The sun is usually up in the sky, aiming down at us here on earth, so put your flash up high on a light stand, and angle it so it's aiming down at your subject. If you're inside, pretend there's no roof. You can see the resulting image from this shoot on the book's website at www.kelbytraining.com/books/digphotogv3.

Which Side Should Your Flash Go On?

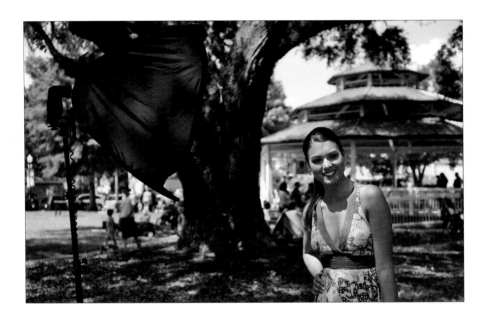

I once heard a famous portrait photographer say he always positions his light on his left side, because back in his days as a news photographer, he used to hold his flash in his outstretched left hand, so he could hold the camera and press the shutter button with his right hand. He's so used to seeing his light from the left, that now, even in the studio, he puts his studio strobe on the left side. I usually light subjects from the left side, too (but I have no idea why—I guess I'm just used to it that way). However, if I'm on location and can't light from the left side, I just move the light to the right side. Not everything to do with lighting has to be complicated. (See page 220 for the final image and recipe for the shoot shown here.)

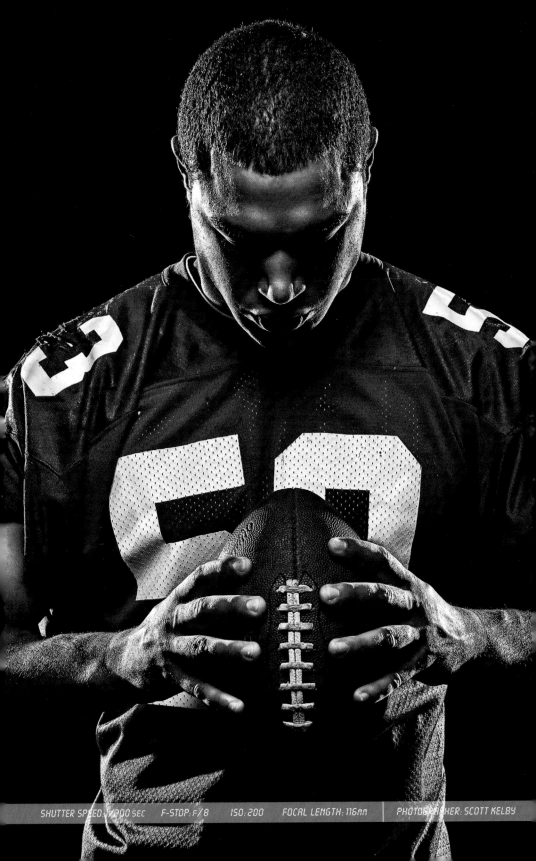

SHUTTER SPEED: 1/200 SEC   F-STOP: F/8   ISO: 200   FOCAL LENGTH: 116mm   PHOTOGRAPHER: SCOTT KELBY

Chapter Two

Using Your Studio Like a Pro

In Volume 2, We Built It From Scratch. Now, Let's Pimp It!

Back in volume 2, I showed you how, using just a simple, thin piece of plastic that fits easily in your wallet, you can completely and fully outfit a one-light studio from scratch. Well, after I wrote that chapter, people who read it wrote me and asked some really thought-provoking and soul-searching questions like, "What if we want to use two lights?" or "What if we want to add a second light?" and even "What if we have one light, but think we might need another?" I'm not gonna lie to you. I was pretty freaked out. I thought we covered so much in volume 2 that there was no way anyone would want to learn more, so when I originally wrote the outline for this book, volume 3, not only did I not have a chapter on more studio techniques, I specifically didn't mention the word studio, or techniques, or use any words with either an "s" or "t" in them, just in case. But then I realized writing a book without an "s" or "t" in it would preclude me from using my first name, and if that happened, I wouldn't be able to refer to myself in the third person (like, "Scott doesn't want to share more studio techniques" or "Scott made bail"). So, I really had to revisit the whole concept with a fresh set of eyes, and once I did, I realized that not only would I have to include a studio chapter that picks up where volume 2 left off, but I would actually have to rebuild my original studio from scratch, because after volume 2 was complete, and the chapter was done, I built a huge bonfire and destroyed all my gear. That's how "done" I thought I was with studio techniques, but apparently, that's not the case. Scott doesn't like to have to rebuild everything. Scott doesn't like to pull out the thin piece of plastic from his wallet. Scott needs a second job.

The Easy Way to a Pure White Background

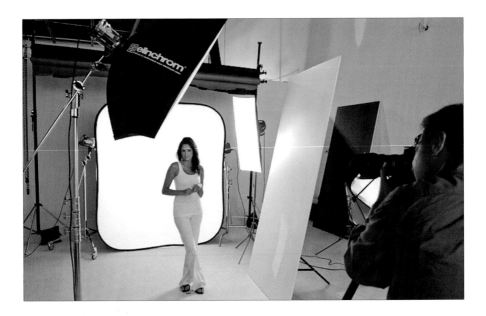

Getting a solid white background (ideal for shooting kids or fashion) can be challenging, because you'll usually need two lights to light it evenly, and you have to worry about balancing the light so there's not a "hot spot," where one side looks brighter. That's why I switched to using Lastolite's HiLite Illuminated Background. Now I have perfect, solid white backgrounds every time (even on location). The HiLite is collapsible, and when you pop it up, you just put a single flash head inside, on either side (or both), and aim it toward the back wall. Then, lower the power of your flash to around ¼-power. Now when you fire your strobe, the light hits the back of the HiLite and evenly spreads out for perfect coverage. There are slots for lights on both sides, but I've used it with one strobe, and it works perfectly—just remember to keep a reflector on the front of your strobe, so it doesn't get too hot. Plus, you can take it on location easily, because it folds up like a large reflector. It takes about three minutes to set up, and is lightweight enough to hold in one hand. To see the final image from this shoot, go to www.kelbytraining.com/books/digphotogv3.

Increase Your Chances of Success With A Shot List

If you're preparing for a studio shoot, take two minutes now and make a shot list—a written list of the types of images you want to create during the shoot. List everything from the lighting setups you want to use, to the poses you want to try, to any props you want to incorporate. When you have a plan, your chances for success go way up!

Strobes with Built-In Wireless Rock!

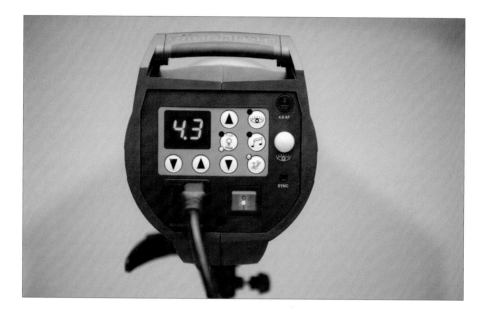

As you can see from the previous page, I'm always looking for an easy way to do... well...pretty much everything (after all, the simpler it is, the more time you can spend shooting, right?). Well, Elinchrom's new BXRi strobes come with a Skyport EL wireless trigger built right in—all you need is the transmitter that slides into the hot shoe on the top of your camera. Besides the fact that the wireless capability is built right into the strobes, there's something I think is even more helpful: you can now control the power of all your strobes from right at your camera using the transmitter. That means if you have a strobe as a hair light up on a boom, and it's too bright, you can just turn down the power while you're right there at your camera—no pulling the boom stand down (or climbing up on a ladder) to change the power on the back of the strobe. It controls up to four different groups of strobes, so you can have one assigned to your main light, one to a hair light, and one to a background light, and control them all without ever leaving your camera. I know—pretty sweet. You can get a kit from B&H Photo with two of the 500-watt BXRi strobes, two 26" softboxes, two light stands, two cases, and the wireless transmitter you need to make it all wireless, and the whole thing is around $1,550, which I think is a steal for this quality of a rig (I have one myself).

Using a Set Background

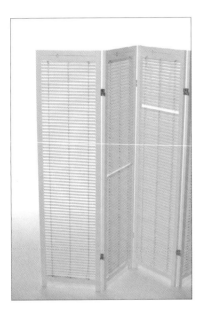
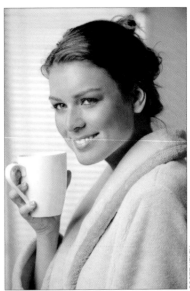

SCOTT KELBY

If you're shooting in the studio a lot, it won't be long before you get bored with shooting on white, gray, and black seamless paper, and the easy way to leverage those is to create your own sets (don't worry—it's much easier than you'd think). Notice I didn't say "build your own sets" (that's too much work). So, to make this work, you'll need to: (1) Go to your local Salvation Army, Goodwill, or thrift store (or keep an eye out at garage sales) for things like room dividers with shutters, large frames, coffee tables, an old couch, lamps on stands, basically just "stuff" to go in the background. It really doesn't matter that much what it is because of #2 and #3. Now, (2) you need to create some depth between your white, gray, or black seamless and your subject, then put your set pieces in between them (so it goes: seamless, a few feet of empty space, then your set pieces, a few more feet, then your subject—to see the setup for the shot on the right above, go to www.kelbytraining.com/books/digphotogv3). Then (and this is key), (3) you need to shoot at a pretty wide open aperture like f/4, or f/2.8, so the background elements are thrown so far out of focus that you can't tell if your shot was taken in a large mansion, or in a bedroom, or in a studio. I'm consistently amazed at how well just putting a few simple things in the background can look when you follow rules #2 and #3. Also, if you find anything you can hang off a boom stand—so it looks like it's hanging from a ceiling in the background—that will help sell the effect big time. Remember, what makes this work is the depth between your background, your set pieces, and your subject, and the very shallow depth of field. You'll be amazed at the results.

You've Got to Have Music During the Shoot

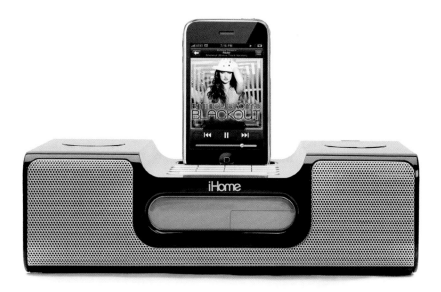

Ask any pro who shoots people for a living, and they'll tell you that they have music on during the shoot. Having that music playing in the background goes a long way toward making the people you're shooting more relaxed and comfortable, which usually trans-lates into better looking images (if they're relaxed and having fun, the photos will look that way, too). All you need is an iPod (or any other portable media player)—go download some songs, get a small iPod-compatible speaker, and you're set. Now, here's the thing: for this really to make a difference, don't just play your favorite music (that will only make you feel relaxed and comfortable), you want to play your subject's favorite type of music. The type that will have them on the set saying, "Oh man, I love this song!" For this book, I shot with a number of professional male and female models, and I'd always ask them what type of music they liked. Sadly, they never choose old school funk or '80s big hair rock, or I would have had them covered. Instead, they wanted the same music they listen to at home and in their car: R&B, hip hop, rock, rap, and alternative. So, I called another photogra-pher I know (my buddy, Terry White) who always has great music playing during his shoots, and I asked him where he got his music. Well, no surprise, he had one of his models pick it out, and he said, almost without exception, he gets raves from models in the studio about his musical taste. He made an iTunes iMix of his collection for me to download, and he was nice enough to let me share that iMix with you. Just go to www.kelbytraining.com/books/digphotogv3 and click on the link, which will launch iTunes and take you to that playlist, where you can buy one or all of the songs with just a click.

The Beauty Dish Look

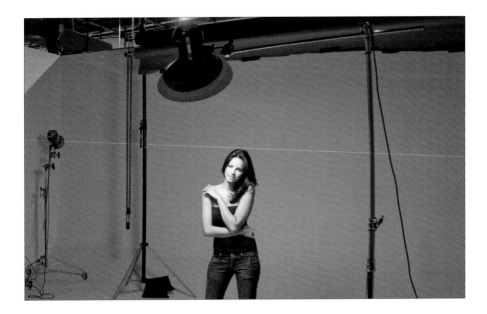

If you want a look that isn't as soft as one with a softbox, but isn't as hard-edged as a bare-bulb strobe, you should try a beauty dish. The light it produces is kind of in between the two, giving you more punchy contrast without getting too harsh or edgy. A beauty dish attaches to the front of your strobe (like a softbox), but it looks more like a giant metal reflector. The light it produces has more "kick," which creates a very nice look for close-up face and headshots (because of the way it defines the face and skin tones), and it's great for anything you want to have that beauty look you see so often in makeup and beauty product print ads. You can also get a "sock" for your beauty dish, which covers the front to give you a little softer look. When you use the dish, it's usually positioned directly in front of your subject, up high, and tilted down at them at a 45° angle (as shown here). You have to kind of shoot under it. You may also want to put a reflector flat at your subject's chest level to fill in the shadows under their eyes (see page 50). Also, depending on which brand you buy (I use a 17" Elinchrom beauty dish), you'll probably have to choose between a white dish interior and a silver one. I chose the white because it's a little softer (the silver is more reflective and contrasty).

Using Grid Spots

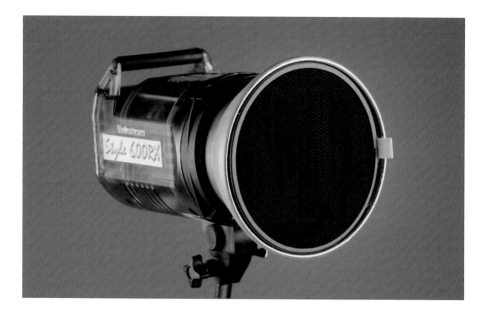

If you took your softbox off your strobe, the light from the flash bulb would pretty much just go everywhere. That's one of the reasons we use softboxes in the first place—to help us put the light where we want it and greatly soften it, of course, but softboxes are, by nature, soft. That's where grid spots come in. These attach right over your strobe's reflector (the kind I use actually snap right into the reflector), and they have a metal honeycomb pattern that gives you a narrow, focused beam for very dramatic effects (the light will be hard-edged, because there's no softbox—it's a bare bulb with a metal reflector and a grid spot). Right now, you see these grid spots used big time as back-edge lights in portraits (in fact, I'm not sure you can find a magazine editorial-style cover shot in the past year that doesn't use at least one, if not two, rear grid spots, putting a white highlight on either side of the subject). These come in different degrees (like a 10° grid, a 20°, and so on), and the lower the number, the tighter the beam (I usually use a 20° or 30° grid). There's not much to using them. You just snap them into place and that's it—your beam is greatly narrowed. Put one on either side of your subject, aim them at the sides of their face, then use a strobe up front to put some fill light into their face, and—voilá—you've got the look. Well, there is a little more to it—make sure you see the last chapter of the book for more on this look—but it all starts with a grid spot.

Shooting Tethered Directly to a TV Monitor

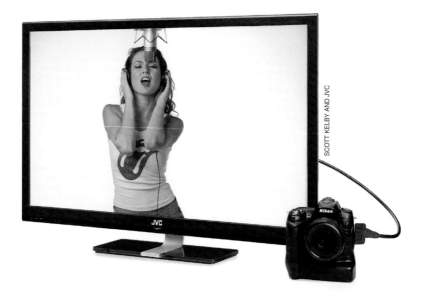

SCOTT KELBY AND JVC

If you want to see a much larger view of what you would normally see on the tiny LCD on the back of your camera, try tethering your camera to a television monitor. Most newer dSLRs have some sort of video output (the newer, high-end Canon and Nikon bodies even have HDMI outputs), so you can take the video cable from your camera, go straight to the input on the television monitor, and see your LCD at a huge size. This is different than tethering your camera to a desktop computer or a laptop, because the images are still being burned onto your memory card (rather than being imported into a computer), and with this type of tethering, the TV monitor does actually take the place of, and do all the same functions as, your camera's LCD screen. So, you can see highlight warnings, see your camera's settings, and everything you would normally see on your camera's LCD, but now you see it huge! I can't tell you how helpful it is to see your images at this large a size, because you can see exactly what the light looks like, you can see exactly how sharp your images are, you'll catch mistakes you'd miss looking at a 2.5" or 3" LCD, and your subjects will love being able to see themselves at this size. I find it really gets them excited when they like what they see onscreen, and that turns into much better images all around. So, what do you need to make this happen (besides the TV, of course)? You'll need whichever cable your particular camera uses as a video out (many dSLRs come with this cable right in the box). That's all it takes.

Getting Your Laptop Nearby for Tethering

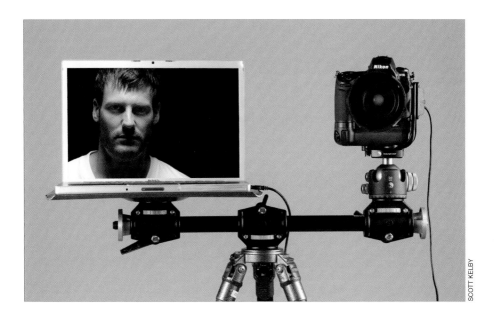

SCOTT KELBY

If you decide you want to tether directly to your laptop, where your images are downloaded into your computer, so you can sort and tweak them as you shoot (I showed how to do this in volume 2), then having your laptop in a convenient spot is real a time saver, and this rig (shown above) is about the easiest and most stable way to get there. It's a metal platform called the Gitzo G-065 Monitor Platform, which screws right into a standard tripod, and it's just the right size for a 15" laptop. If you often shoot using a tripod, then you can have this one tripod do double-duty by adding a Manfrotto 131DD Tripod Accessory Arm for Four Heads. This is a horizontal bar that screws onto your tripod, then you can attach the Gitzo Monitor Platform with your laptop on one end, and on the other end, you can put the ballhead that would normally be alone on your tripod. This way, one tripod holds them both, and they're right there together. Pretty sweet!

Judging Your Image Quality Onscreen

Here's something to keep an eye out for: when you open your image on a large-screen computer monitor (24" or larger) and view it at 100%, chances are it's not going to look tack sharp, but keep in mind that you're seeing it at a "larger than life" size. Zoom out until the size you see onscreen is approximately the physical size you plan to print the image. If you plan to print the image at a large poster size, make sure you back up at least six feet from the monitor to see the image at the same view everybody else views large images.

The Most Useful Inexpensive Accessories

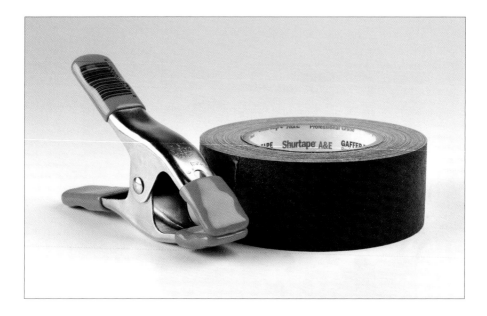

If you don't have a roll of gaffer's tape in your studio, put down this book, go online, and order a few rolls right now. Not duct tape. Not electrical tape. Gaffer's tape! It's one of those
things that once you have it, you'll wonder how you got through a shoot without it (ask any
studio photographer). You'll use it for everything from holding grid spots in place, to fixing a
gap in a softbox, to keeping things together when doing product shots, to...I could go on
and on. The other thing you need about six, or so, of are A-clamps. They're another one of those
things that should be in every studio, and you'll use them for everything from hanging things
from a boom stand, to pinning back clothing on your subject to get rid of wrinkles (which
is why you need small ones and large ones). You'll find these at your local hardware store (or
go online) and you'll find a hundred uses for them. Keep these two inexpensive accessories around, and you'll keep from pulling your hair out—and it'll keep the shoot moving
ahead (instead of coming to a halt while you run to the store).

Why You'll Love Rolling Light Stands

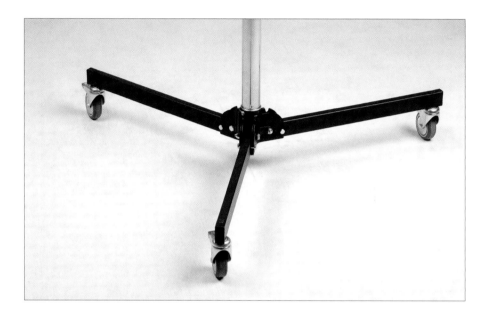

At some point, you're going to wind up buying light stands for your studio, so here's a bit of advice that will make life in your studio much easier: buy light stands with wheels. There are two big reasons you'll want to do this: One is pretty obvious—you'll be moving your lights a lot, and it's much faster and easier to roll them around than pick them up and move them. Plus, I've found (and I've seen firsthand with other photographers) that you're more likely to move your lights, and experiment, if they're on wheels. The second advantage is safety. Lights are top-heavy, and all the weight—the strobe, the softbox, and any accessories—is at the top of the stand. When you pick one up to move it, it's easier to bang it into something, or lose balance and topple the whole rig over, than you'd imagine (believe me—I've seen it). Whatever it costs you for wheels, you'll make back quickly by avoiding repair bills, potential injuries on the set, and visits to the chiropractor.

Why You Need Sandbags

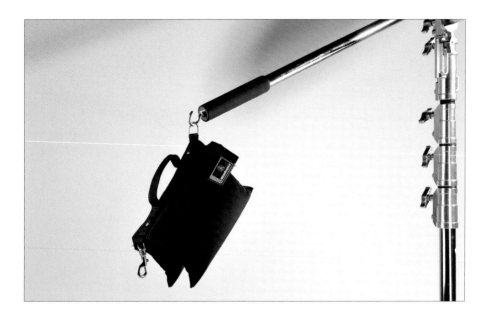

I don't care how sturdy a boom stand you buy, one day (probably soon), it's going to go crashing over. The best-case scenario is that it just breaks your strobe's bulb, or the strobe itself, or maybe just tears your softbox. The worst-case scenario is that it falls on your subject, your client, a makeup artist, or a friend. It's not a matter of *if* it happens—it's like a hard drive crash—it's a matter of *when* it happens. That's why you absolutely need to have some sandbags, and to use them religiously when you've got anything on a boom or if you take anything outside on a shoot (where the wind can blow it over). B&H Photo sells empty sandbags—when they arrive you just fill them with sand (you can also find some pre-filled bags, but prepare to pay for shipping them). You can find them at your local hardware store, as well. Once you get them, put them on the legs of your boom stand to balance the weight, or hang them off the boom arm to add a counterweight (as shown above), or both, and take a big worry off your big worry list. Another thing to watch out for: be careful when removing your sandbags, because if the weight of them is keeping the boom from tipping over, when you remove the sandbag, your boom could topple right over. So, just keep an eye (or a hand) on things when you're taking them off.

Monolight vs. Battery Pack

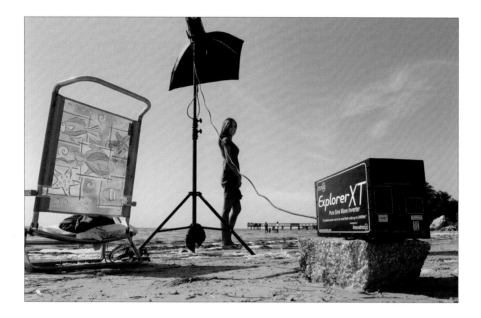

A monolight (also sometimes called a monoblock) is just a regular studio strobe that you plug right into a wall socket like a regular lamp. If you want to take studio strobes out on location, instead you use a battery pack and special strobe heads made to run off batteries (for example, I use an Elinchrom Ranger kit, which is a battery pack and strobe head). The advantage of something like a Ranger kit is you can take your studio lighting outdoors (to the beach, in the desert, out on a boat, etc.), but the disadvantage is you have to use special "made for the battery" strobe heads. However, now more and more companies are selling battery packs that let you plug your regular studio strobes right into them (for example, I've been using a battery pack called an Explorer XT, from Innovatronix, that lets me plug in up to two of my regular studio strobes, and it was fairly affordable compared to dedicated packs—around less than half the price). So, instead of having to buy strobe heads and a battery pack, if you already own studio strobes, all you have to buy is the battery pack. Sweet!

One Background, Three Different Looks

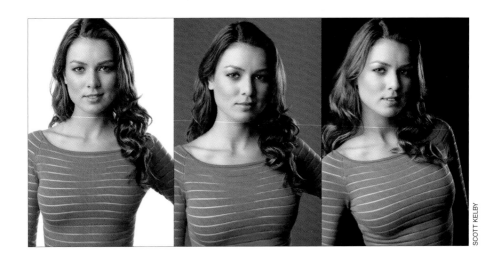

SCOTT KELBY

One nice thing about buying a white seamless background is, depending on how you light it (and what shutter speed you use), you can get three different looks. Here's how:

(1) To have a white background, you have to light it, so position a light (or ideally one on each side) down low, aiming up a bit to light the background. That gives you white.

(2) To have a gray background, just turn the background light(s) off. White paper needs light not to look gray, so when you turn those lights off, it gives you gray—your second color from the same white background.

(3) To get a black background, leave the lights off, and increase your shutter speed to as high as your camera will allow (your maximum sync speed), which is probably 1/200 or 1/250 of a second. This makes your background go even darker—to at least a very dark gray or a solid black—just by changing the shutter speed. What you're essentially doing is, by raising the shutter speed, you're eliminating any light already in the room (called "ambient light").

Using a Ring Flash

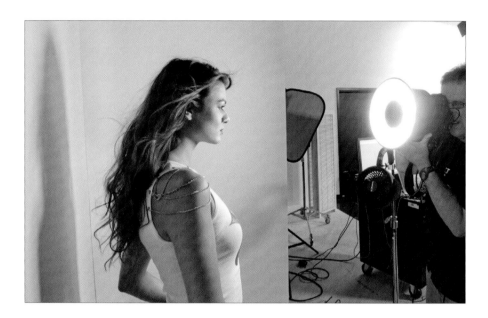

The hot look right now for fashion photography is to use a ring flash, which is a series of small flashes that form a circle around your lens, and give a very flat look with a fairly hard shadow behind your subject. In the chapter on flash (Chapter 1), I showed an adapter you put on your small off-camera flash to imitate a ring flash look, because ring flashes can be pretty expensive. However, I found one that's reasonably priced for someone who's not going to be making their living as a fashion photographer, but sometimes wants that flat, ring flash look. It's the AlienBees ABR800, and it's not terribly heavy (as ring flashes go—they are fairly bulky and heavy by nature), but works surprisingly well considering its $399 price tag (you can spend over $1,000 on a ring flash pretty easily). You can check out page 223 for a photo taken with the AlienBees ring flash, so you can see the type of look you can expect from one.

Using V–Flats for Fashion

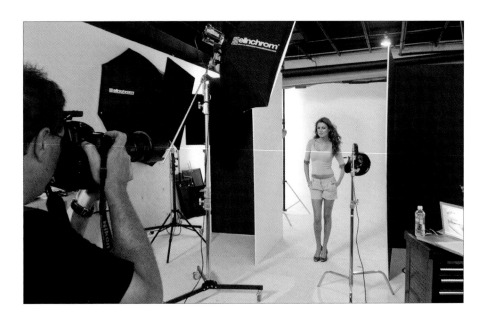

If you're shooting fashion, you're probably going to be shooting a lot of ¾-length and full-length shots, and if that's the case, you'll probably want to get some V-flats (these are actually large foam core sheets that are approximately eight feet tall by three or four feet wide, and you can usually find them with one side black and one side white). You'll use the white side as a giant full-body reflector, placed either directly to the side of your subject (on the opposite side of your main light), or in front and little bit to the side, leaning back a bit to throw some light back toward your subject. The reason these are called V-flats is because you take two of them, form a large V-shape, and tape them together on the seam. That way, you can stand them up and position them where you need them, without having to use a stand of any kind. Also, since one side is black, you can use the black side as a flag (to keep background lights aiming forward at your subject from spilling through to the camera and creating lens flare), or you can face the black side toward your subject, which subtracts light from the scene and gives a dramatic edge to your subject. To see the resulting image from the shoot above, go to the book's website at www.kelbytraining.com/books/digphotogv3.

Catch Lights and Why You Want Them

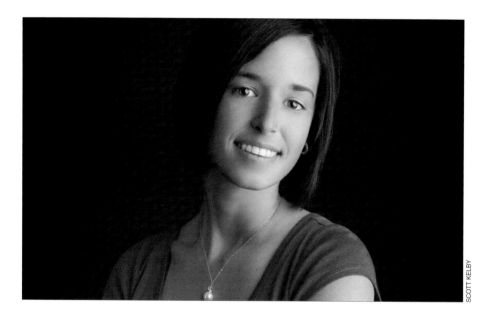

SCOTT KELBY

You know that reflection of your softboxes that appears in your subject's eyes? Those are called catch lights, and you want them. Badly. Without them, your subject's eyes won't have any sparkle to them and will look like dead, lifeless pools of despair (okay, that's pushing it a bit, but you get the idea). So, don't freak out, or as I've had people suggest in emails to me, try to remove them in Photoshop. Instead, make sure they're there, because they're supposed to be there. Now, that being said, the next time you see another studio photographer's work, take a good close look at the subject's eyes and you can usually not only tell which type of softbox they used (square, round, an umbrella, an octagonal softbox, a beauty dish, etc.), but you'll also be able to see the position of the light (if they had it right in front, over to the side, etc.). And, if you see another catch light at the bottom of the eye, you'll know the photographer used a reflector positioned down low to put some light back into the eyes. It's kind of a mini-lighting lesson each time you take a close look.

Reflectors: When to Use Silver or White

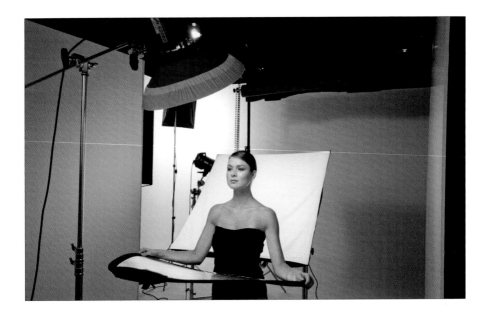

Reflectors come in different colors, but probably the most popular are white, silver, and gold (although gold is usually used outdoors, because adding warm yellow light in with white studio lights usually looks kinda weird). So, that leaves silver and white—which do you use when? Here's the general thinking on this: Silver reflects much more light, so you'll use silver when you position the reflector back away from your subject. If you need to get a reflector right up close, that's when I'd use white, because it doesn't reflect nearly as much light as silver. (See page 231 for the final image from this shoot.)

Reducing Glare in Glasses

If your subject wears glasses, seeing a reflection of the softboxes in their glasses is not uncommon, but you don't want such a strong reflection that it interferes with or covers their eyes. If that's the case, just move the main light to the side until the reflection goes away (it's easier than you'd think, because you'll see the modeling light reflecting in their glasses). However, what's important is that the glare is gone from the angle where your camera is set up, not from where you're standing moving the light. So this will go quicker if you have a friend or assistant move the light while you stand at the camera and tell them, "keep going…keep going…" until you see that the reflection is gone.

Using a Gray Card to Nail Your Color

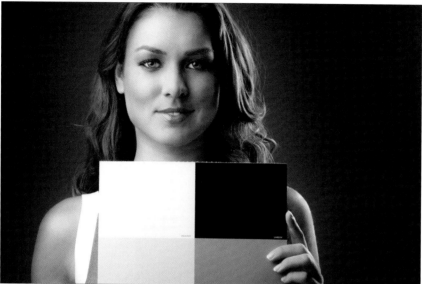

SCOTT KELBY

If you're going to be post-processing your images using a program like Photoshop, or Photoshop Elements, here's a trick that will make the color correction process absolutely painless, and nearly automatic. Once you get your lighting in place, have your subject hold up a gray card target that has medium gray, light gray, black, and white on it (the one shown here is a target that comes free with my book, *The Adobe Photoshop Book for Digital Photographers*), then take a shot with it clearly in the frame. That's it—you need just one shot with the subject holding the card. Now, when you open your photos in Photoshop (or Elements), open the Levels dialog, click on the gray Eyedropper that lives in the dialog, and click it on the medium gray color swatch. Then click the black Eyedropper on the black swatch, the white Eyedropper on the white swatch, and that's it—you've color corrected that photo. Now you can open any other photo taken in that same lighting setup, and press Command-Option-L (PC: Ctrl-Alt-L) to apply that exact same color correction to this new photo. You can also use this same card for adjusting just the white balance of a RAW photo. Open that same photo in Photoshop's Camera Raw (or Photoshop Lightroom's Develop module) and get the White Balance tool from the Tool-box (or the Basic panel), then click it once on the light gray color swatch, and now your white balance is set. You can now apply that same white balance to all your RAW photos by copying-and-pasting just that white balance setting to as many photos as you want at once. A huge time saver.

Don't Light Your Whole Subject Evenly

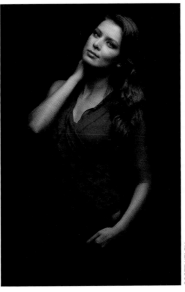

SCOTT KELBY

The first two things the human eye naturally focuses on in a photo are the brightest part and the sharpest part of the photo. Keep this in mind when you're shooting in the studio or on location (even with small off-camera flash), because if you light your entire subject evenly, you won't be directing your viewers to look where you want them to, which in most portraits is the subject's face. For a more professional look, you want their face to be perfectly lit, and then the light should fade away as it moves down their body. How much it fades away is up to you (it can fade to black if you want, but again, that's your call), but when looking at your photo, it should be clear by the lighting where you want people viewing your image to look. One way you can control the light is to position it so it doesn't light all of your subject evenly, or to use a fabric grid, so the light doesn't spill everywhere, or even to use something to block the light from lighting the person's whole body evenly. I use a black flag (a 24x36" cloth flag) and position it under the light (usually on a boom stand), so the light is mostly concentrated on my subject's face. It doesn't have to block all of it—unless I want the person's body to fade to black—it just has to cut down the amount of light that falls on the rest of them. Take a look at your favorite portrait photographers, and you'll see this lighting technique used again and again to create interest, focus, and even drama in their images.

The Difference Between Main and Fill Light

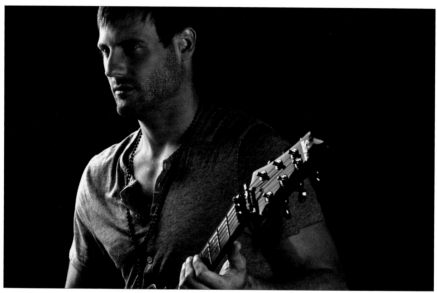

SCOTT KELBY

When working with more than one flash, you've probably heard the terms main light (also called key light) and fill light. Here's what those mean: Whichever flash you choose to do most of the lighting of your subject is the main light. It's as simple as that. If you use another light that is not on the background, or on the subject's hair, *and* the flash isn't as bright as your main light, that's the fill light. The fill light is usually used to add just a little extra light to your scene. For example, let's say you're doing a profile shot of your subject. The profile light goes to their side, and a little behind them. Most of the light appears to come from behind and just a little bit of light falls on the side of their face that faces the camera. But what if it still looks a little too dark? Well, that's when you might add another flash in front (I'd put it opposite the flash behind them), but you'd lower the power of this flash way, way down, so just a little bit of light appears—just enough to fill in those shadows (to see the setup shot for this, go to www.kelbytraining.com/books/digphotogv3). That's a fill light, and now you know the difference between the main light and a fill light.

Avoiding the Flash Sync Speed Black Bar

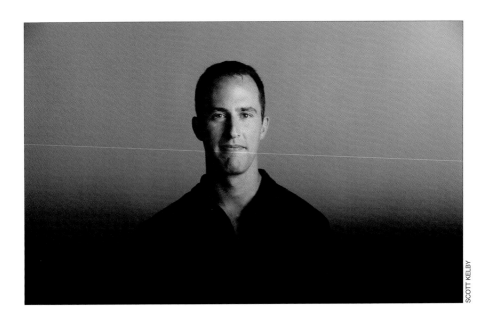

SCOTT KELBY

If you're shooting in the studio, or with an off-camera flash, and you start seeing a black bar, or black gradient, across the bottom or either side of your photo, that's because you're shooting at too high a shutter speed for your camera to sync with your flash. Generally, the flash sync speed (the maximum shutter speed your camera will sync with a flash) is either 1/200 or 1/250 of a second (depending on the make and model of your camera). So, if you see that dreaded black bar, just lower your shutter speed to 1/250 of a second or slower, and that should take care of it.

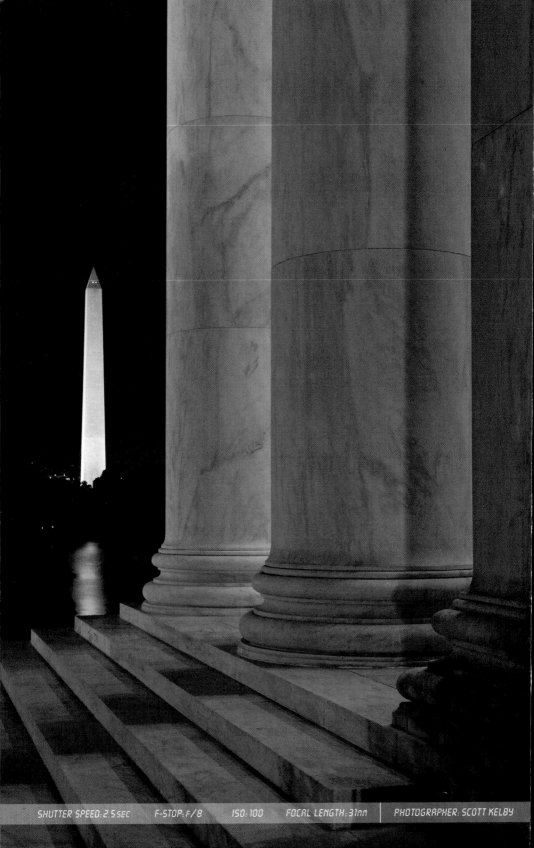

SHUTTER SPEED: 2.5 SEC   F-STOP: F/8   ISO: 100   FOCAL LENGTH: 31mm   PHOTOGRAPHER: SCOTT KELBY

Chapter Three

The Truth About Lenses

Which Lens to Use, When, and Why

One of the questions I get asked most is, "Which lens should I buy next?" Of course, I have to ask a question of my own before I can answer that question, and that is, "How stable is your marriage?" I ask that because if you have a really stable marriage—one that's based on trust, caring, compassion, and a healthy fear of handguns—it's entirely possible that it can endure having one of you become a serious photographer. Otherwise, I refuse to answer the lens question, because having a serious photographer in the family is going to seriously test the strength of your marriage. For example, there will come a day when you'll be faced with the decision of whether to get that new super-sharp, fast f/2.8 lens or to stay married. That's because, in most marriages, one spouse controls the funds, and it should never be the spouse that's into photography, because there will come a day, mark my words, where you'll be holding your mortgage payment book in one hand and the B&H Photo catalog in the other, and you're going to be faced with a moral dilemma that will test the very mettle of your commitment to your spouse, family, and friends. You'll start to ask yourself crazy questions like, "How would we do living on the streets?" and "Would our friends sneak us food?" and "I wonder if they'll throw in a free polarizing lens?" These are not the kinds of questions you want to be asking yourself at this stage of your life (by the way, the more expensive the lens, the more free stuff you should try to get thrown in). Anyway, if one day you're faced with one of these really tough decisions, I'll give you the same advice I gave my own daughter, "Honey, you can always find another husband, but a great sale on some really fast glass only comes along once in a lifetime." (I didn't say those exact words, but it was definitely implied.)

When to Use a Wide–Angle Lens

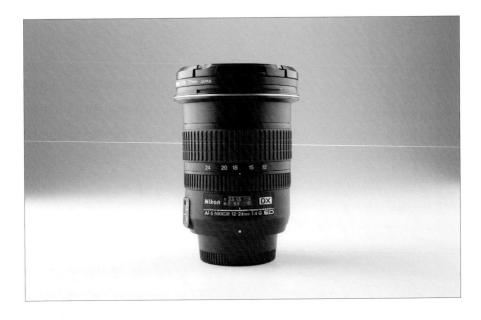

A regular wide-angle lens (as opposed to a "super wide") is around 24mm to 35mm, and it's just about a must if you're shooting landscapes, because the wide aspect takes in more of the scene (think of how much more wide-screen video takes in—it's kind of like that). Wide angle is also very popular for shooting environmental portraits (the type of images you see in magazines when they're doing a feature on a celebrity, politician, or a business exec, where the portrait takes in a lot of their surroundings). For example, if you're shooting a fireman in the fire station, with wide angle, you include a little, or a lot, of a fire truck in the shot, as well. They're also great anytime you want to create a view of something—just get in real close and things get interesting. You can buy wide-angle zooms (which are what I prefer) that zoom from wide-angle to normal (like a 24–70mm), or even a super-wide zoom that goes from 12–24mm. I GRAB THIS LENS FIRST WHEN...I'm going to shoot landscapes using a non-full-frame camera body.

Scott's Gear Finder

Wide-Angle AF Nikkor 24mm f/2.8D Autofocus Lens (around $360)

Canon Wide-Angle EF 24mm f/2.8 Autofocus Lens (around $310)

Sigma 28mm f/1.8 Lens (around $380) [for Nikon, Canon, and others]

When to Use a Fisheye Lens

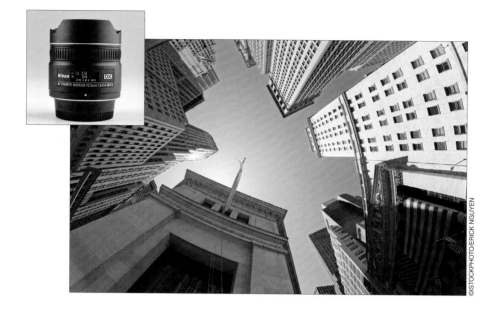

©ISTOCKPHOTO/ERICK NGUYEN

These are well named, because they give you an incredibly wide, almost circular view (and the lens itself bulges out like a fish's eye, but honestly I don't know if the lens was named for how the lens looks, or for how the photo it takes looks). This is definitely a special-effects lens that you want to use occasionally, because the fisheye look can get old fast if you use it too much. However, in the right circumstance, it looks really fasci-nating (try holding it up high over your head when you're in a crowd, or at dinner in a restaurant, and shooting straight down). One thing about fisheye lenses is that they do distort the horizon line quite a bit. For the minimum amount of distortion, try to keep the lens level in front of you, but if you want more creative looks, then all bets are off— just have fun with it. I GRAB THIS LENS FIRST WHEN…I'm going to be in a crowd, when I'm shooting up high in a sports stadium and want to take the whole thing in, or when I'm shooting skyscrapers and want to get them all.

Scott's Gear Finder

Nikkor AF 10.5mm f/2.8 Fisheye Lens (around $700)

Canon EF 15mm f/2.8 Fisheye Lens (around $660)

Sigma 10mm f/2.8 Fisheye Lens (around $700) [for Nikon, Canon, and others]

When to Use a Telephoto Zoom

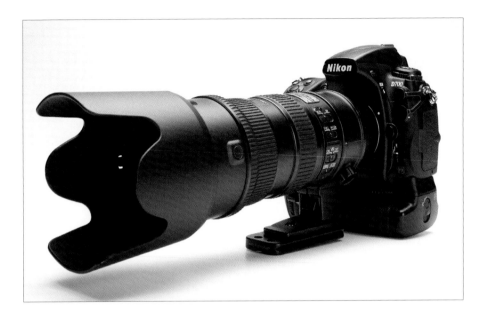

When you want to get up close and in tight, this is the ticket. Now, you could just get a telephoto lens (one where the length is fixed, like a 200mm telephoto), and not a tele-photo zoom (where you can zoom in from one length, like 80mm, all the way through to a really close view, like 300mm), but then if you hold the camera up and you're either too close, or too far away, your only option is to physically move up close, or back up. With a telephoto zoom, you can simply zoom in tighter, or zoom out if you're too close, which makes all the difference in how you'll compose your shots. I use telephoto zooms for everything from portraits to sporting events to architectural shots (I prefer to zoom in and focus on an interesting aspect or individual part of the building, rather than trying to show the whole thing at once). I GRAB THIS LENS FIRST WHEN...I'm shooting portraits or sports.

Jump Start Your Creativity By Using Just One Lens

The next time you're in a creative rut, try going out shooting and use just one lens the entire day (or if all you have is a zoom lens, try picking one end of the zoom [wide] or the other [telephoto] and shoot at that one focal length the whole day). Not having the lens you need for a particular shot forces you to get creative.

When to Use Super-Fast Lenses

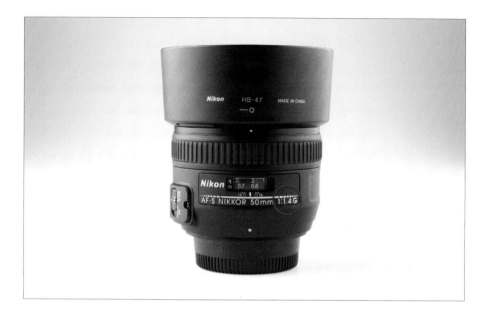

If you want to shoot indoors without using flash (like in a church, museum, theater, or anywhere flash and/or tripods aren't allowed), then you need a really fast lens (which just means a lens whose f-stop goes to a very low number, like f/1.8 or, better yet, f/1.4. The lower the number, the lower light you'll be able to shoot in without using a tripod). Here's why this is so crucial: when you shoot in a dark place, the only way your camera can make a photograph is to slow down your shutter speed, so more light makes its way into your camera. That's not a problem if your camera is mounted on a tripod, because it's perfectly still, however, if you're hand-holding your camera (which is going to be the case in almost every church, museum, etc.), and your shutter speed falls below 1/60 of a second, you're going to have photos that look okay on the back of your camera, but when you open them later on your computer, or have them printed, they will be incredibly blurry and basically unusable. So, by setting your camera to f/1.8 or f/1.4, you'll be able to hand-hold in lots of places and have sharp, clear images where normally they'd be blurry as heck. In this case, less (a lower number) is more. I GRAB THIS LENS FIRST WHEN...I'm shooting a wedding.

If You're Really Serious About Getting Sharper Images, Try This Trick!

You can use the same technique sharpshooters (with rifles) use to minimize any movement while firing—they hold their breath. That's right. When hand-holding, some pro photographers only shoot after they exhale (or they take a deep breath and hold it, then shoot). This minimizes body movement, which minimizes camera shake.

When to Use an Ultra-Wide Zoom Lens

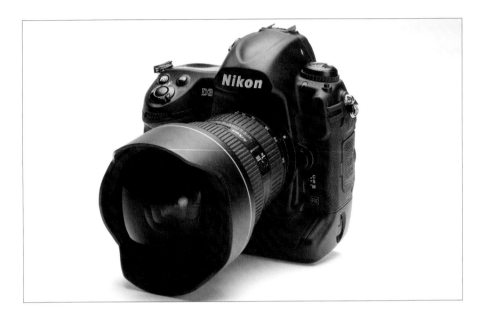

Although you see this lens used in creative ways for everything from portraits to travel photography, this is really a lens born for landscape photography. In fact, it's so wide it may be the ultimate lens for landscape photography (if you're a DVD or Blu-ray movie buff, think of a super-wide-angle lens like anamorphic wide screen). These lenses go as low as 12mm, and my favorite is my 14–24mm f/2.8 lens. If you find a lens below 12mm (like an 11mm, or 10.5mm), it usually means that it's a fisheye lens (see page 59), so I would stay away from that for most serious landscape work. Now, if you have a dSLR with a full-frame sensor, and you use a wide-angle zoom that's made for full-frame sensors (like a Nikkor 14–24mm f/2.8), it will capture a much wider image than it would if you used that same lens on any regular dSLR that isn't full frame (see page 72 for more on full-frame vs. regular), or if you used a regular lens on a non-full-frame camera. (This is where full-frame cameras really shine—when you want to go wide. In fact, when it comes to lenses, wide-angle is probably where you see the biggest improvement, because you get a really, really wide view with full-frame cameras.) I GRAB THIS LENS FIRST WHEN...I'm shooting landscapes.

When to Use a Super-Telephoto Lens

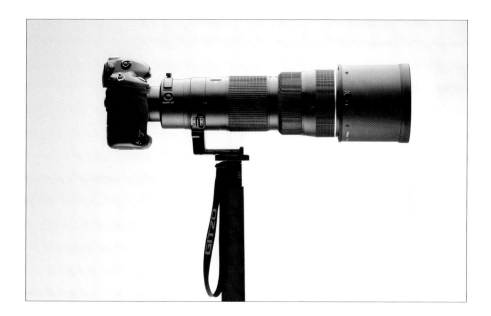

We call this "the long glass" (because the lens barrel itself is often very long), and it's designed to get you in really tight on whatever you're shooting. Typical focal lengths for these lenses would be from around 300mm up to around 600mm (or higher). They are mostly used for sports photography, aerial photography, and for shooting wildlife and birds. You can buy fixed focal lengths (like a Canon 400mm f/5.6), but they also make super-telephoto zoom lenses, as well (I use a Nikkor 200–400mm f/4 zoom myself). If you want a lens that will shoot in lower light (like an f/4 or an f/2.8), it can get really pricey (for example, the Canon 500mm f/4 lens runs around $5,800)—they're so expensive because the very low f-stop lets you shoot in lower light, like a night game, and still freeze motion. However, if you generally shoot sports in the middle of the day, in nice bright sunlight, then you can get away with buying a less expensive super-telephoto lens (like the Canon zoom telephoto EF 100–400mm f/4.5–5.6 for around $1,460). Also, if you buy a long lens, you're usually going to need a monopod to support it (your monopod screws into a hole on a bracket on the lens, and your camera is supported by being attached to the lens. It works much better than it sounds). I GRAB THIS LENS FIRST WHEN...I'm shooting sports.

Using a Teleconverter to Get Even Closer

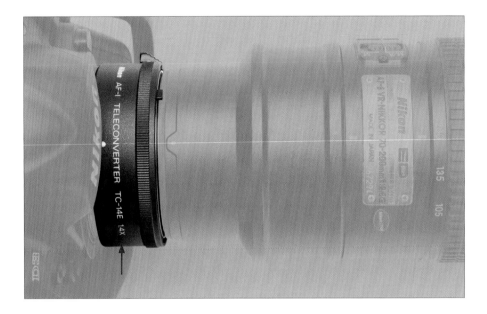

I talked briefly about teleconverters back in volume 1, because they're such a handy and relatively inexpensive way to get you in tighter to the action. What these do is zoom your whole lens in a little closer, usually either 1.4x closer, 1.7x closer, or even 2x closer (though I only recommend the 1.4x teleconverter, because the quality doesn't change noticeably like it does with a 1.7x or 2x extender). As long as you buy a quality teleconverter (both Nikon and Canon make very good ones), there's only one potential downside, and that is you lose around one stop of light for a 1.4x (more for higher ones). So, if the lowest number your lens would go was f/2.8, when you add a teleconverter, now the lowest number is f/4. I say potential downside, because if you shoot in broad daylight, losing a stop of light isn't a big problem for you. But, if you shoot under stadium lighting at night, then it's a problem, because you can't afford to lose that stop of light—it might mean the difference between sharp shots and blurry movement. I GRAB A TELECONVERTER FIRST WHEN...I'm shooting sports or wildlife in bright daylight.

Teleconverters Don't Work with Every Lens

Before you buy a teleconverter, make sure it works with your lens—not every lens will work with a teleconverter. Look on the order page for the teleconverter and it will usually list the lenses that it either will or won't work with.

Lenses with VR or IS Built In

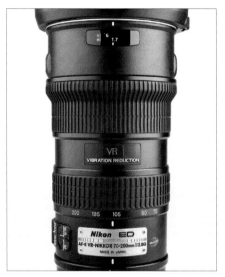

Nikon

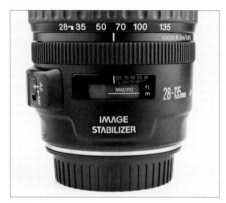

Canon

Lens manufacturers know that people have a hard time hand-holding their cameras in low-light situations, so they started adding features that automatically help keep the lenses from moving, so you get sharper shots in low light. Nikon calls their brand of this "anti-movement" technology VR, for Vibration Reduction, and Canon calls theirs IS, for Image Stabilization. They're both well-named, because that's what they do—they hold your lens steady for you, so you get sharper shots, but it really only makes a difference when you are shooting at a slow shutter speed (you'll get no improvement when you're shooting in broad daylight, because your shutter speed will be so fast [which freezes any motion], that there's no reason for VR or IS to kick in). What VR and IS do is let you hand-hold in lower light situations, so if you wind up shooting a lot in churches, museums, theaters, and other low-light locations, you should probably keep an eye out for VR or IS lenses (they usually cost a little more). Also, you won't often find this feature in already very fast lenses, like an f/1.8 or f/1.4. One more thing: if you're shooting on a tripod, you should turn VR or IS off (there's a switch on the lens) to reduce any shake caused by the VR or IS searching for movement.

Using Active VR for Nikon Users

If you're a Nikon shooter, your VR lens may have a setting called Active, and that only needs to be turned on when what you're standing on is moving (if you're shooting from a boat, or a moving car, or a suspension bridge, etc.).

Using Filters with Your Lenses

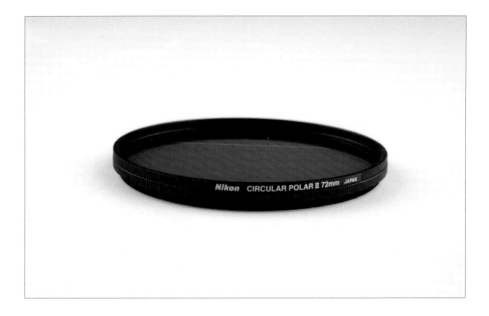

There are literally hundreds of different filters you can slap on the end of your lens to either fix a problem (like to help you capture something your camera can't expose properly for) or create a look, but I only own three filters, and one of them I don't really use as a filter (more on that in a moment). They are:

(1) A Neutral Density Gradient Filter. This is mainly for people shooting landscapes, and it fixes a problem that happens when you expose for your foreground in a landscape shot and the sky gets totally washed out. You put this in front of your lens, and it darkens just the sky, so the sky looks right and the ground in front of you looks right (see Chapter 5 for more on this filter).

(2) A Circular Polarizer (shown above). Another landscape filter, and one no landscape photographer should be without. While it's designed to greatly reduce reflections in things like lakes and streams, which it does brilliantly, most folks use it to darken the sky. It's like putting a pair of sunglasses over your lens. The world looks less annoyingly bright.

(3) A UV Filter. Technically, this filters out unwanted UV rays from your lens, but what we all use it for is to protect our lens from getting scratches on it. Putting this filter on puts a thin piece of glass between your lens and anything that would scratch, or worse yet, break it. They're very cheap, so if one breaks or gets scratches, you just replace it. Life goes on. Get a scratch on one of your lenses, and they'll hear you weeping six blocks away. I buy a UV filter for every lens I own.

The Deal on Lens Hoods

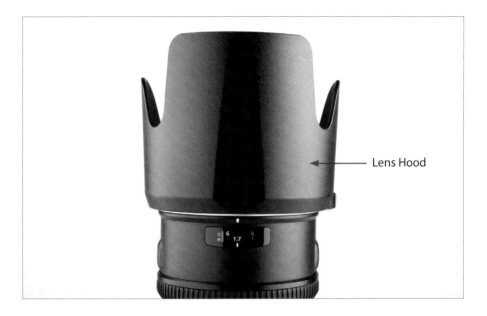

Lens Hood

Besides making your lens look longer and "more professional," a lens hood serves two very important roles (one advertised, one not as much). The first is that the lens hood helps keep lens flare from the sun, or from a flash, from getting to your lens and washing out your photos. Most good quality lenses these days come with a lens hood that is specifically engineered to work with that particular lens. The other, less publicized, use is to protect your lens from getting scratched or broken while it's slung over your shoulder as you walk around. I can't tell you how many times I've banged my lens against a chair, the end of a table, even a wall when coming around a corner, but all I ever hear is the sound of plastic, and it bouncing right off. If I didn't have a lens hood, I'm certain I would have had a number of scratched or broken lenses, but so far—not a one. I keep my lens hood on all the time. Besides, they look cool (don't tell anyone I said that). By the way, you can turn your lens hood around, facing back toward you, when storing it in your camera bag, or when it's not in use. I GRAB A LENS HOOD...anytime one comes with my lens, and I keep it on always.

When to Use a Macro Lens

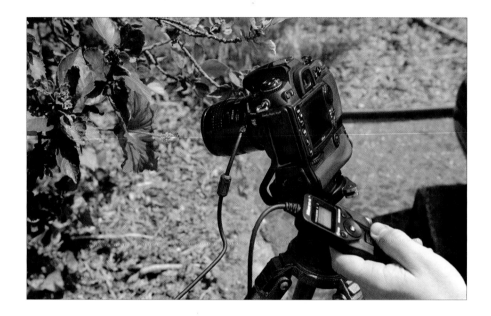

This is the lens you pull out when you want to shoot something really, really close up. Ever see those photos of bees really close up, or flowers, or ladybugs? That's macro. Dedicated macro lenses just do that one thing, but they do it really, really well. There are a few things you need to know about macro lenses:

(1) They have an amazingly shallow depth of field. So shallow that you can be shooting a flower, and the petal in the front will be sharp and in focus, and a petal on the other side of the flower will be so out of focus you can barely make out what it is. That shallow depth of field is one of the things that I love about macro lenses, but it's also a challenge when you're trying to get more things in focus (try shooting at f/22 to get as much in focus as possible. Also, try keeping your lens horizontal and not angling the lens up or down when you shoot for a little more depth).

(2) Any little movement or vibration will mean an out-of-focus photo, so I definitely recommend shooting on a tripod if at all possible. Using a cable release of some sort, so you don't actually have to touch the camera (possible vibration maker), will also help (see volume 1 for more on cable releases).

When to Use a Tilt-Shift Lens

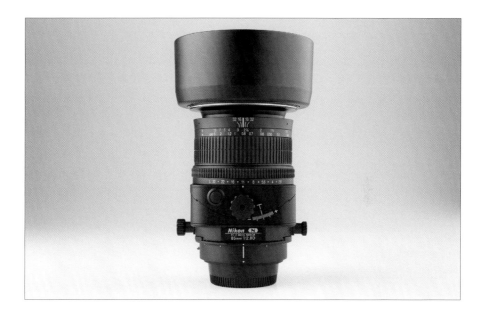

This is a specialty lens if there ever was one! This is used primarily for shooting architecture, because you can shift part of the lens itself to keep your buildings from looking distorted as they climb upward. Serious architectural photographers swear by these, and many won't shoot architecture without them. Of course, like any specialty lens—they're not cheap.

If You Buy a Filter, Make Sure It's the Right Size for Your Lens

The filter you buy has to fit your particular size lens (some lenses are larger around in diameter than others, so you have to make sure the filter you order is the same size diameter [measured in millimeters] as your lens). For example, my 18–200mm lens takes a 72mm filter, but my 70–200mm lens takes a 77mm filter. Want a great way to quickly find out the right size? Go to B&H Photo's website (www.bhphotovideo.com), find your lens, and you'll see a bunch of filter accessories listed below it. They will display the size used for that lens. Also, if you bought one filter and want to use it on a slightly different sized lens, you can sometimes buy a step-up or step-down ring adapter that will let you do that, and it will still work just fine.

How to Clean a Lens

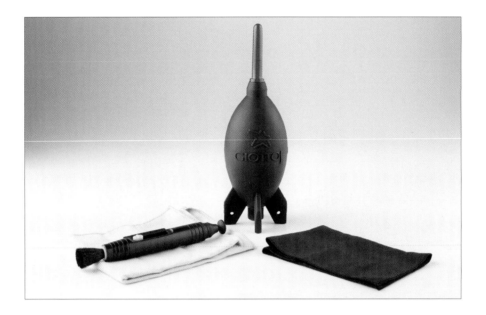

If you get some dust, a smudge, dirt, etc., on your lens, something really bad is going to happen—that dust, or smudge, etc., is going to appear on every single photo you take with that lens. All of them. Every one! That's why it's important to clean your lenses before you go shooting for the day, and anytime you see a little "junk" on your lens. Most of the time, you can use a simple lens cleaning cloth, but before you do that, it's best to first start by blowing any junk off the face of your lens (you can do that by just blowing with your mouth, but ideally you'd use a little hand-squeeze blower bulb), and then once any visible specks and dirt are blown away, you can clean the lens with the lens cloth by gently rubbing in a circular motion. You can get a lens cleaning kit for around $15, which includes a blower, a cleaning cloth, and particularly helpful is one that includes a LensPen, which has a little fine brush on one end, and a special cleaning tip on the other end. It works wonders.

Long Lenses Usually Come with Lens Collars

When you buy a long lens, they usually come with a special bracket on the bottom that lets you attach a monopod, but there's something else you'll love about these brackets that's not apparent at first: unscrew one little knob and you can instantly rotate your camera to a vertical shooting position, while the lens stays put. This lets you switch from shooting wide to shooting tall in all of two seconds.

When to Use the Manual Focus Ring

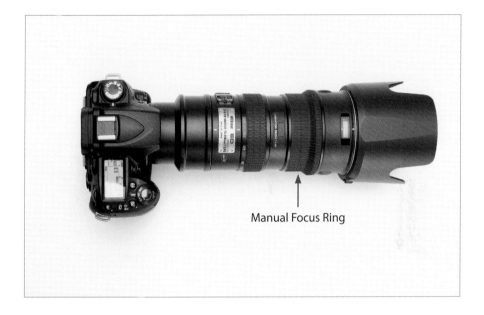

Manual Focus Ring

Most lenses let you turn off the autofocus feature and manually focus your lens, but a lot of today's lenses actually let you do both: start by letting autofocus set your initial focus, but then override it and tweak your focus using the manual focus ring (usually found at the far end of the lens). There are photographers who do this every time (start with autofocus and then tweak it), but most (like myself) just rely on today's excellent autofocus capabilities to do the work for them. If you want to tweak the focus yourself using the manual focus ring, just let autofocus do its thing first, and lock onto your subject before you start tweaking the manual focus ring.

Buying a Really Fast Lens for Studio Work

Over the years, I've run into so many photographers who have spent a ton on really fast lenses (like f/2.8 and f/4 lenses—usually the faster the lens, the more they cost), yet they either primarily, or only, shoot in the studio. This is just pretty much tossing money down the drain, because they probably rarely, if ever, shoot at f/2.8 or f/4 because they're not shooting in low-light situations (after all, they're in a studio—if they want things to be brighter, they just increase the power of their strobes). I guess the moral of this story is: if you don't shoot in low-light situations, you don't need expensive, really fast glass. Save your money for other studio gear and accessories (see, you thought I was just going to say, "Save your money," but I had already allocated your savings to other fun stuff, like studio strobes).

Zoomed vs. Full-Frame Lenses

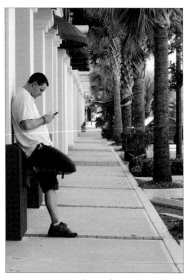

Zoomed

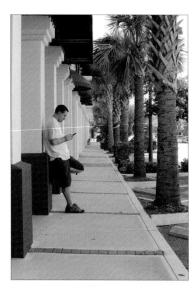

Full-Frame

You've probably heard by now that most digital cameras (and dSLRs) have a zoom factor. What that means is that the number of millimeters you read listed on the lens used with a digital camera is different than what you used to get with a traditional 35mm film camera. For example, if you put an 85mm traditional lens on a digital camera, it's not really 85mm. On a Nikon, the lens is zoomed in by a factor of 1.5, so your 85mm lens is really giving you the results of a 127mm lens. On Canon cameras, it's zoomed in by 1.6, so an 85mm lens is really more like a 135mm lens. This drives photographers who have moved from film cameras to digital cameras a little nuts, because to them, an 85mm should be an 85mm, but that's just the way it's always been. However, now the big buzz is around full-frame cameras, and what that means is that with full-frame cameras, an 85mm is an 85mm once again. There is no zoom factor, no multiplication—the lens is finally really what it says it is. Ahhhh, but there's a gotcha! (Isn't there always?) If you put a lens that was made for a stan- dard digital camera (and most digital lenses are just that) on a full-frame camera, it zooms it (basically, it crops your photo down to the zoomed dimensions). What that means to you and me is if you buy a full-frame digital camera, you won't get the advantage of a full- frame camera (at least when it comes to lenses), unless you buy lenses that are specially made for full-frame cameras. Now, that being said, some of the higher end, more expensive lenses do work fine with full-frame cameras and they don't crop down the image. So, how do you know which ones do and which ones don't? I put together a partial list for Nikon and Canon users at www.kelbytraining.com/books/digphotogv3.

Lens Vignetting and How to Remove It

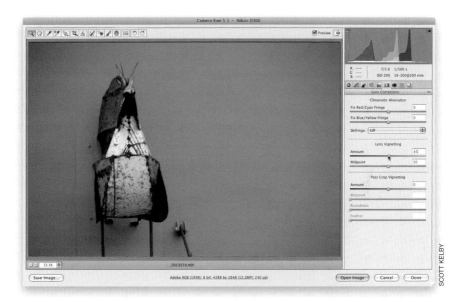

SCOTT KELBY

Have you ever taken a shot, and then when you look at the shot on your computer, you notice that the corners of your image seem darker than the rest of the photo? It's a fairly common thing, especially with some wide-angle lenses and some of the less expensive lenses. This is called "edge vignetting," and it is a problem caused by the lens itself that winds up on your photos. Luckily, you can remove edge vignetting (also known as lens vignetting) in most image editing programs, like Photoshop, Photoshop Lightroom, Photoshop Elements, etc. For example, in Photoshop's or Elements' Camera Raw window, you can click on the Lens Corrections tab and you'll see a section for removing lens vignetting. Drag the Amount slider to the right to lighten up the corners. The Midpoint slider below it determines how far into the photo the lightening extends, so if it's just right up in the corners, you can drag the slider quite a bit to the left. If the darkening extends pretty far out into your photo, then you'd drag to the right. In just a few seconds, your vignetting problem is gone! If you use Lightroom, you have the exact same controls, which work exactly the same way, in the Develop module. Just scroll down to the Vignettes panel. If all this sounds a bit confusing, don't worry—I made a quick little video just for you to show you what edge vignetting is and how to remove it. You can find it at www.kelbytraining.com/books/digphotogv3.

Why Some Lenses Have Two f-Stops (Like f/3.5–5.6)

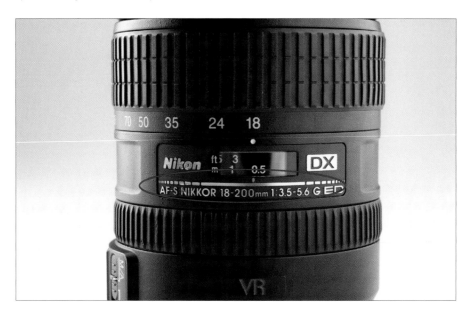

When you see a zoom lens that has two different f-stops, what that means is that at the short-er range (let's say it's an 18–200mm lens, so we'd be talking about when you're at 18mm), the f-stop can go as low as f/3.5, but when you zoom it out to 200mm, the fastest it can go is f/5.6. When you're in between the two, the f-stop will gradually increase (so at 100mm, you might be at f/4). What this tells you is two things: (1) If you shoot at the wide-angle end (18mm), you'll be able to shoot in much lower light than you can zoomed in at 200mm (the lower the f-stop of the lens, the darker light you can hand-hold your camera in and still get sharp photos). This also means (2) that this is a less-expensive lens. Really "good glass" (as it's called) has a constant aperture (the same f-stop all the way through the zoom range), so the lens would be at, say f/2.8, whether you're out at wide angle or zoomed in tight (for example, Nikon's 70–200 f/2.8 VR lens can shoot at f/2.8 whether you're zoomed out at 70mm or zoomed in tight at 200mm).

When You Need to Focus Really Fast, Turn the Focus Limit Switch On

Each time you use autofocus, your lens searches everything it sees, from a few inches in front of you to miles in the distance, and then it locks on what it thinks you're aiming at. This takes just a second or two, but if what you're shooting is really far away (you're shoot-ing sports or a bird up in a tree), you can switch your lens from Full focus to Limit, which tells it not to even try to focus on anything closer than around eight feet away. That way it focuses even faster, so you don't miss the shot.

Tips on Changing Lenses

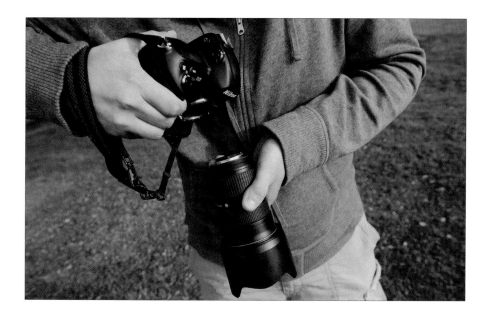

If you have more than one lens, you'll probably be changing lenses in the field quite a bit, and if so, there are just a couple of things you should know. The first is that you generally don't have to turn the camera off to change lenses. Although you'll read some purists online who claim having the sensor still charged will attract dust and blah, blah, blah, I don't know any pros who actually turn their camera off to change lenses. However, when you do change your lens, to keep dust from actually falling into your camera itself, don't leave the open body of the camera facing straight up. That's just askin' for it. You're better off tilting the body down toward the ground. Also, if you're in a dusty or windy environment (let's say you're shooting in Arizona's Antelope Canyon slots, where dust is constantly trickling down from the above), don't change lenses at all—wait until you're in a clear area first, and then do it. And, ideally, you don't want to leave your camera body uncovered for long (again, to keep out dust), so don't take five minutes changing lenses—take one off, and pop on the other. You don't have to rush (you don't want to risk dropping anything), but don't dilly-dally either. (There's a term you don't hear every day.)

What to Do If Your Autofocus Suddenly Stops Working

First, check to see that you didn't turn off the autofocus on your lens, but if it's on, try this: just remove the lens, and then put it right back on again (called "reseating the lens"). This little trick has worked for me time and time again.

When to Use an "All-in-One" Zoom

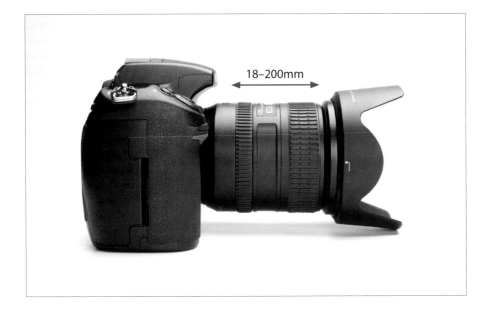

The most popular Nikon and Canon lenses are their 18–200mm zooms, because they do it all. They go all the way from a nice wide angle to a tight telephoto and you never have to change lenses at all. Best of all, they're compact, pretty lightweight, and relatively inexpensive compared to some of the more expensive zooms with a smaller range. These are ideal lenses for travel photography (where you don't want to lug a camera bag around with you all day), or for photo walks, for city shooting, and even for landscapes you'll be shooting on a tripod. I have one of these 18–200mm lenses and, honestly, I love mine dearly. Now, you will see some photographers in forums online saying that these lenses are basically beneath them, because they're not as sharp as they could be, or they're not as rugged as the more expensive lenses, etc. Don't let that throw you. I don't know a single photographer that actually has one of these that doesn't love it, mostly because when it's on your camera, you're never going to say, "Oh, I missed that shot because I didn't have the right lens," because it does it all in one lens. As for quality, I have a 30x40" print of a photo I took with that lens while on vacation, framed, and hanging in my home. Everybody loves it, and it looks perfectly sharp and crisp all the way through. I GRAB THIS LENS FIRST WHEN...I'm going on vacation.

When to Use a Lensbaby Lens

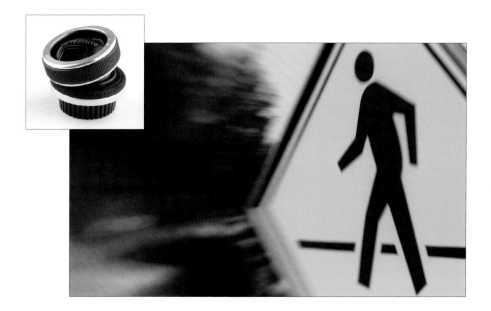

Before I tell you about this lens, I have to warn you: people get hooked on Lensbaby lenses, and I can't tell you how many times a photographer friend I've known has bought a Lensbaby and then won't take it off their camera. They shoot everything, from the birth of their child to a space shuttle launch, with it, because these lenses (which you focus and aim with your thumbs and forefingers) are just plain addictive. So, you know that going in. Lensbaby lenses give you one small area of your photo that is sharp and in focus, and then all the other areas around that sharp area quickly go way out of focus and blurry, which results in a look that can have a lot of energy, movement and excitement to it. Of course, the look is only part of it, because what really gets people hooked on it is that whole "move it yourself" thing. It just feels like you're really "making a picture," rather than just taking a picture. I GRAB THIS LENS FIRST WHEN...I'm in the mood to shoot something really creative.

What Makes It a Portrait Lens?

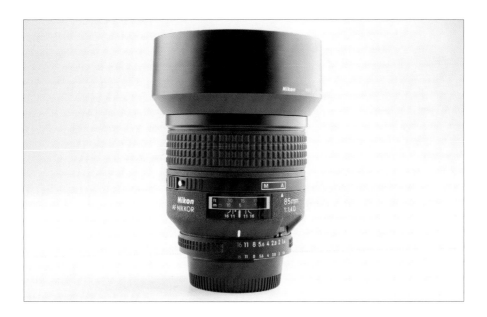

There are certain lenses that have been referred to as portrait lenses, and I always get asked, "What's a good portrait lens?" That's a good question, and one that doesn't (like many things with lenses) have a single definitive answer. I would say that generally a portrait lens would be a fixed-length lens (so it doesn't zoom) that is between 85mm and 105mm. But, here's the problem (and where a lot of the mental fuzziness comes in): Back on page 72, I talked about the zoom factor and full-frame cameras. So, an 85mm fixed-length lens on a regular non-full-frame digital camera is actually more like a 120mm lens, right? See what I mean? That being said, you may remember that back in volume 2 I talked about how much better portraits look when shot with a longer lens because of the compression longer lenses give, which looks more flattering to the face (I showed a side-by-side comparison in the book). That's why you'll see so many fashion and portrait photographers shooting with 70–200mm lenses, and they're frequently out at the 200mm range for head or head-and-shoulders shots (especially if the model has dandruff. Sorry—I couldn't resist). I have shot with 85mm lenses on full-frame cameras, but I didn't like the look as well as I do an 85mm on a regular digital camera, so for my style, I like the 120mm range better. If you use a telephoto zoom, you can try both and see what you like. My point is you don't have to buy a portrait lens (whatever that means to you) to take pro portraits. Today's zooms do a beautiful job, and as long as you're over 100mm, I think you'll be pleased with the results.

Fixed-Length Prime Lenses vs. Zooms

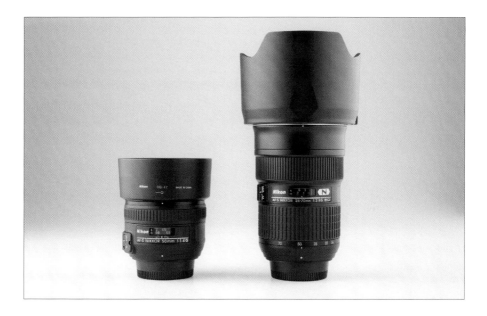

You have to realize one thing about lenses—people get really "techie" about lenses, and they are a source of constant debate in online forums, where people get really conde-scending about which lenses they will or won't use. One current debate is prime lenses vs. zoom lenses. There are people who swear that fixed-length lenses (lenses that don't zoom—they are one particular length, and that's it—and are more commonly called a "prime lens") are visibly sharper than zoom lenses. I truly believe that at one point in time, this was absolutely the case. Zoom lenses were lesser quality, and primes were sharper (and generally they did, and still do, let you focus up closer). But I personally don't think that's the case with today's higher-quality zoom lenses (not just any zoom, but a high-quality zoom, like one that's f/2.8 all the way through). I think there are but a handful of photographers who, with the naked eye, can tell whether you took a par-ticular shot with a zoom lens or a prime lens. I think it's more of a perceived difference, not an actual difference, but again, this is what creates these drawn out debates. This is going to send people who want to believe there's a big difference into a rage, but I've talked directly with manufacturers who make both the prime and zoom lenses them-selves, and they've told me, point blank, that with today's higher-quality zoom lenses, there is no visible sharpness difference between zooms and primes. That being said, I do own two prime lenses. They are both very sharp. So are my good zooms. Either way, this isn't something to get hung up on. It's just a lens. Not a religion.

Shooting at Your Lens' Sharpest Aperture

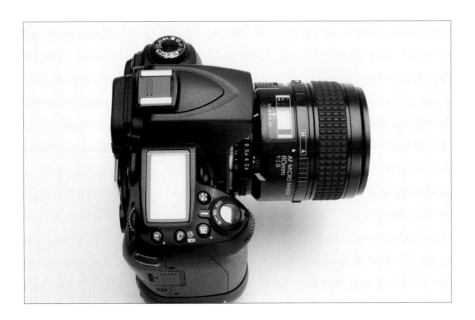

I mentioned this in volume 1, in the chapter on getting really sharp photos, but I couldn't do a chapter on lenses and not include this really important technique. In short, each lens has a sweet spot—a particular aperture where the lens takes the sharpest image it can take. Where is that sweet spot? Usually, it's two stops above the lowest number your lens can go. So, for example, if you have an f/2.8 lens, then its sweet spot would be two stops above that, at f/5.6. Will your photo look sharper at f/5.6 than it will wide open at f/2.8? Yup.

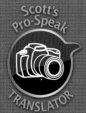

When talking about lenses, if you hear the term "wide open," that means that you're shooting at the smallest number on your lens, like f/2.8 or f/4. Of course, you could just say, "I was shooting at f/4," but it doesn't sound nearly as cool as saying, "I was shooting wide open at f/4." Hey, you're snickering now, but wait until you're at one of those at-home lens parties, and you casually drop a "wide open" in there. You'll see the hostess drop her lens hood.

But My Friend Has That Lens and He Shoots...

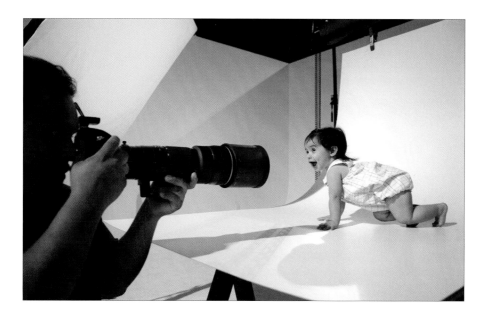

It's bound to happen. You're going to have a friend who's a serious photographer, and you'll hear that he's using a fisheye lens to shoot executive portraits or a 400mm super-telephoto lens to shoot baby photos. Then you're going to say, "But Scott said fisheyes aren't for portraits, and you should use a portrait lens for babies!" Here's the thing: if you buy any one of those lenses, you're going to try it out on other stuff. In fact, you should—it's your lens and you should try it on as many things as you'd like. That's half the fun of it. You may find yourself enjoying taking fisheye shots in a courtroom, and tilt-shift lens shots of your kid's high school graduation. In fact, your tilt-shift lens may become your go-to lens for shooting graduations, and there's nothing wrong with that. What I hoped to do in this chapter is send you in the right direction and give you a starting point for what type of lens is commonly used for what, but because it's a lens, it will take a photo of anything you aim it at when you press the shutter button. So, don't feel bad (or feel it's wrong) if you use a lens that's commonly used for one thing on something completely opposite. There's a name for doing stuff like that: creativity. Have fun with it, and don't get put aside by all the lens bullies. It's your lens. Fire away!

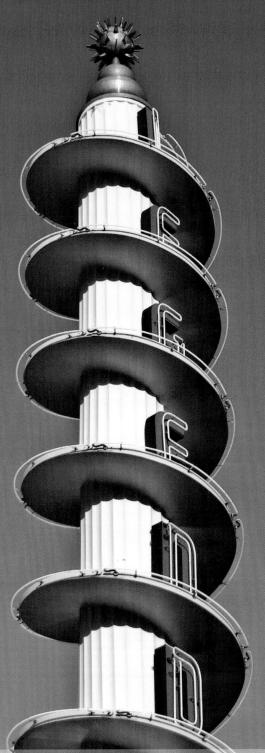

Chapter Four

Shooting Products Like a Pro

How to Get Them to Look Like You've Always Wanted Them To

The first time you look at this chapter, you might think to your-self, "Why would I need to know how to make a great photo of a product?" There are tons of reasons (shooting products is surprisingly fun), but the most obvious might be having a great product shot is critical if you're selling stuff on eBay.com. Now, you might be thinking, "But I'm not selling any stuff on eBay," and if you just said that, that tells me one thing—that this is the first chapter of the book that you turned to, because although this book wasn't designed to make you want to buy new stuff, the sad truth is, to get the same results the pros get, sometimes you have to buy stuff (sometimes it's an accessory, or a light, or a filter, etc.). The stuff might not cost a lot, but still, it's stuff you have to buy. Okay, so if it's stuff you have to buy, some of it will probably be replacing stuff you already have, right? For example, if you bought a digital camera "kit" (where you got a camera body and a lens together), then when you read the chapter on lenses, you're undoubtedly going to see a lens you're going to want. But then you'll think to yourself, "I don't really need that lens. The lens I have is fine." But the more you think about it, the more you start to think, "If I sold my old lens, and some other camera gear I don't use anymore, I could probably buy that new lens," and then you figure that the easiest way to sell your old stuff is to sell it on eBay (which was practically invented for photographers), and so now you think, "I need to do a product shot," and it's at that moment that you realize you've been sucked into the whole photography equipment merry-go-round. Once you're on it, it's easier to come off drug addiction, because they actually have rehab centers for drug dependency, but there is no rehab clinic for photographers, which is why the best thing you can do is just skip this chapter and get on with your life. See? I care.

How to Create Real Reflections

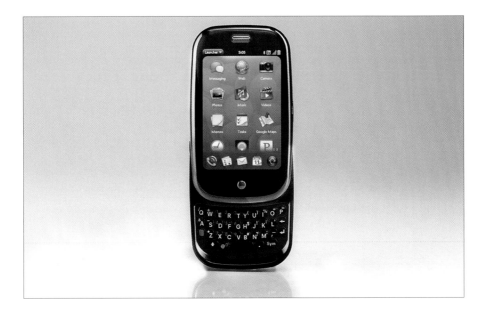

In professional product photography, you'll often see a reflection appear below the product, and while you can add these reflections after the fact in Photoshop, it's easier to just have real reflections (plus, depending on the angle of the product, the job of creating fake reflections in Photoshop can range anywhere from quick and easy to a real pain in the %*$#, so you're better off doing it right up front). The easy way to get those reflections is to shoot your product on some plexiglass (either clear or white frosted). Just put a rectangular sheet of plexi right over your background (you can pick up these small sheets of plexiglass at your local Home Depot or Lowe's for around $15) and it does the rest. Plus, plexiglass is handy for all sorts of other stuff (you'll see it used again in a couple of pages, and another in Chapter 10. To see a production setup using plexiglass, go to page 93).

Faking Reflections in Adobe Photoshop

If you need to fake a reflection, here's how it's done: Make a selection around your product, then press Command-J (PC: Ctrl-J) to put that product up on its own separate layer. Go under the Edit menu, under Transform, and choose Flip Vertical. This turns your product upside down. Now press-and-hold the Shift key, and drag your product straight downward until the two "bottoms" touch, then in the Layers panel, lower the opacity of this layer to around 20%. That's it!

Mirrors for Those Hard-to-Light Places

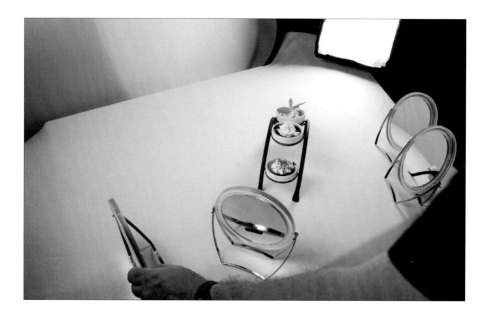

When you're shooting products, it's very important to make sure the product is really well lit, and sometimes it's hard to get into little nooks and crannies with your light, which is why you'll love this trick: buy a few little tabletop mirrors (the kind they sell at the local pharmacy or Walmart, but make sure they tilt). Position a couple of these right outside your frame, aim them directly at the area you need to light, and they will reflect your studio light into those areas (if you're using continuous light for your product photography, like I talk about on page 88, then you'll be able to use these mirrors like little spotlights— as you tilt the mirror back and forth, you'll see a small beam of light that you can aim right where you want it. The first time you see this, you'll be amazed. If you're using strobes, it's a little trickier, but what you can do is turn up the power on your modeling lights and then use that light to aim the mirrors. Just know that when you fire your strobe, the amount of light you're putting into those shadow areas will be much brighter). The great thing about these mirrors is they're inexpensive, lightweight, and small enough to throw in your camera bag or lighting gear case.

Buying Your Little Mirrors

Make sure you don't buy too large a mirror, because you don't want to have to shoot around them, so keep them no larger than four inches around. Also, if you choose a mirror with a magnifier on one side, you'll have two different looks for your light.

Lighting From Underneath

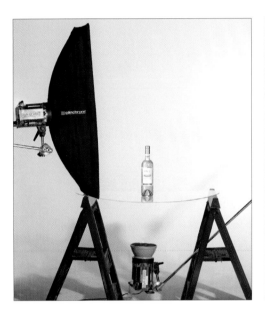
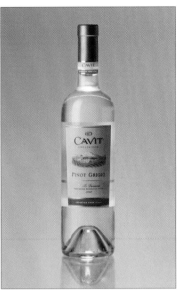

A really popular technique for lighting products is to include a light coming from below the product. You see this look fairly often in product photography, and if you're shooting a product that has see-through areas (like glass), it really looks great. Okay, so you're probably wondering how you get that light through the table to your product. Plexi-glass! Instead of setting your product on a white background (and then putting the plexiglass on top of it), you remove the white background, and use your plexiglass as the tabletop (if you're going to be doing this often, make sure you buy thicker plexi from the hardware store). Just suspend the plexiglass between two light stands (or even between two sawhorses or two chair backs), and then position a light directly under the plexi-glass—on the floor—aiming upward through it.

Concentrating Your Below-Product Light

When you're lighting from underneath, you really don't want your light to spill out every-where—you want it concentrated straight upward. One way to help with that is to use a grid spot attachment (see page 39), which focuses your beam, but a lot of folks will just put foam core or black flags around all four sides of the light, so the light doesn't spill out. I've even seen DIY projects where you put the strobe on a short stand inside a cardboard box, and then you cut a little door out so you can reach in and adjust your strobe.

The Advantage of Shooting Inside a Tent

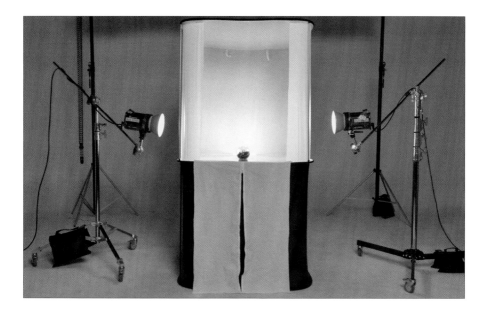

Product tents have become more popular than ever, because they allow you to easily wrap balanced soft light right around the product, while avoiding lots of nasty shadow problems you're likely to run into using multiple lights. Shadows are really a problem and soft light is a problem, so having a self-contained tent like this makes shooting the products crazy easy. The idea behind these is you put a light on both sides or either side of the tent (and perhaps one light below, aiming straight up, if you buy one that includes that feature, like the Studio Cubelite from Lastolite, shown above), and then the front of this is open for you to shoot. The light bounces around inside this box in a very wonderful way that lights the living daylights out of your product, and you come away with some surprisingly good results without having to be a master of lighting. If you're going to be doing a lot of this, and especially if you're trying to shoot things like watches or jewelry, you should definitely consider buying a light tent.

Using Continuous Lighting

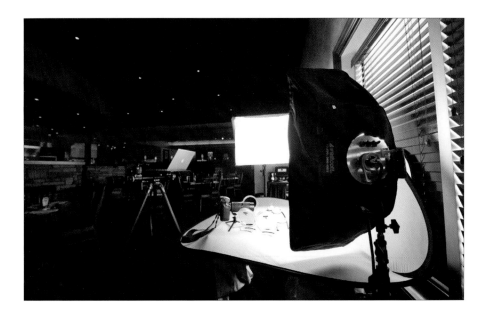

Although I've used strobes many times over the years for product photography, today when I need to shoot a product, I usually use continuous lights like the Westcott TD5 Spiderlite. These aren't flashes, these are lights that stay on all the time, and they give bright daylight-balanced light, but because they use fluorescent bulbs, they don't get hot, so you can even use them to light food (as I did in the restaurant shoot above). These work incredibly well for product photography, because you can see exactly what you're going to get—there's no shooting a few shots, and then tweaking the lights, and shooting again, and tweaking the lights, because exactly what you see is what you get. Outside of the fact that they stay on all the time, they're just like strobes, and have all the similar accessories, like softboxes in every size (including strip banks), and fabric grids, and all the other stuff, but since they're always on, you don't have to worry about a wireless trigger or flash cables. I always recommend these to my friends, and everybody I've recommended them to has fallen in love with them. You can pick up a one-light kit (which includes the fixture, a softbox, tilt bracket, and light stand—bulbs need to be ordered separately) from B&H Photo for around $530. You can also get the fixture on its own (for around $280), but again, the bulbs need to be ordered separately.

Mixing Daylight and Studio Lights

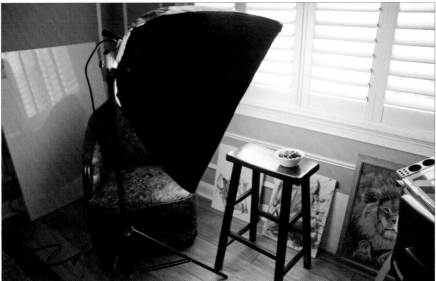

SCOTT KELBY

If you've got a lot of space with a lot of natural light, you can shoot just using the natural light, but the problem is going to be getting light to wrap all the way around your product. That's why adding one light, and mixing that with your natural light, can make a big difference. I do this a lot when shooting food, or wine bottles, where I use the natural light for the backlighting (so it's really the main light) and then I use a West-cott Spiderlite continuous light for a fill light in front (after all, if the light is coming from behind my product, the front of the product will be kind of a silhouette. Bringing a little light in from the front makes all the difference in the world). The advantage of the Spiderlite is that it's daylight-balanced, and mixes really well with natural daylight. (To see the final image from this shoot, just go to the book's companion website at www.kelbytraining.com/books/digphotogv3.)

Enhancing Highlights and Shadows in Post

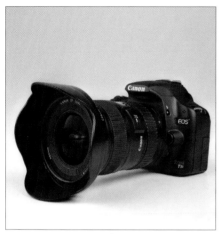

Before

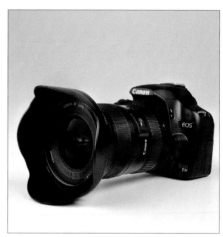

After

Although we always strive to get as much right in the camera as possible, product photography is one area where it usually pays to do a little tweaking in Photoshop after the fact
(called "post-processing" or just "post" by people who can only use one word at a time). When
I shoot a product, what I'm looking to do in Photoshop (besides removing any specks, dust,
or other little junk on the background or the product itself) is to enhance the highlights
(the brightest areas of the product) and the shadows (the darker areas). Basically, I make the
highlights brighter and more obvious, and the shadow areas a bit darker and richer. Once
you see the difference this makes, you'll want to be doing some "post" yourself. I did a little
video for you (you can find it on the book's companion website at www.kelbytraining.com/
books/digphotogv3) to show you exactly how the Photoshop post-processing was done for
most of the product shots used here in the book. I think you'll be surprised at both how easy
it is, and what an impact it has on the finished image.

What File Format to Save Your Photos In

Even though we shoot in RAW format, once you open and edit your photos in a program
like Photoshop, at some point, you're going to have a duplicate of the same image (for uploading to a lab, or archiving, etc.), and that's when you have to decide which file format to
save your images in. I choose JPEG mode with a quality setting of 10 (out of a possible 12)
for all my final images (I think a setting of 10 gives an ideal balance between maintaining
great quality and still compressing the file size quite a bit).

Making Your Own Product Table

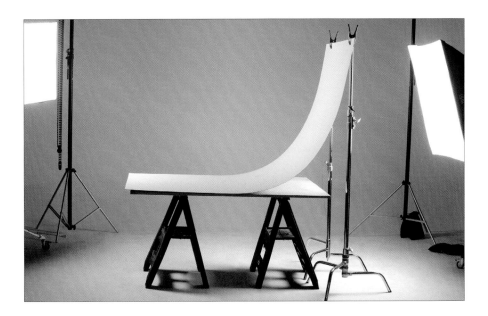

If you're looking for a great surface to shoot your product shots on, look no further than your local hardware store for a large panel of white formica. This stuff works great for a number of reasons: (1) When you put a product on white formica, its surface is already a little reflective, so it automatically gives your product a little bit of a natural reflection (not a sharp mirror reflection like acrylic, but kind of a subtle satin-like reflection). (2) It's very easy to keep clean—you can just wipe it lightly with a damp cloth—so you don't have to replace it often, like you do with white seamless paper, and (3) because it bends pretty easily, you can lie one end flat on a table, and then attach the other end to a couple of inexpensive light stands with some A-clamps (see page 42 for more on A-clamps), and this gives you a smooth, seamless curve behind your product, which makes it perfect for product photography. A full 8x4' sheet costs about $45–50 at my local hardware store, and believe it, it's worth every penny.

Special Wire for Hanging Products

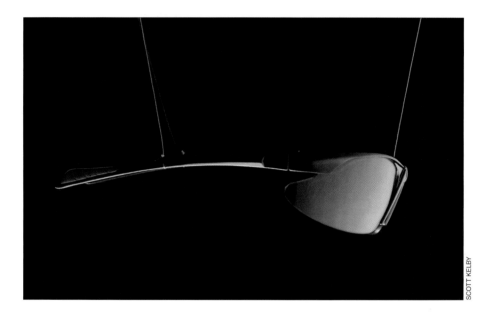

SCOTT KELBY

Invisible thread. It's not just for repairing your clothes—this incredibly sturdy stuff can be used to suspend products in midair so you can shoot them (well, of course, it depends on the weight of the product. It's not going to hold a car battery, if that's what you're thinking). Just put a boom stand arm up high—just high enough so you can't see it in your viewfinder—then tie one end of the invisible thread to the boom, the other end to your product, and fire away. Now, you can also use fishing line if you can't get hold of some invisible thread, and while it's pretty unobtrusive, you're probably going to have to remove that line later in Photoshop. That's what I used in the shot you see above, and I did a video clip on how I removed the fishing line using Adobe Photoshop (the clip actually aired on *Photoshop User TV*, a weekly video podcast I've been co-hosting for the past few years), and you can see that clip on the book's companion website at www.kelbytraining.com/books/digphotogv3.

The Advantage of Using Strip Banks

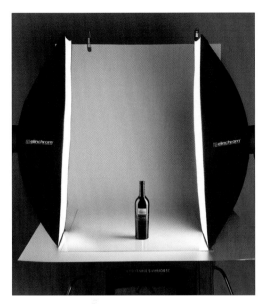 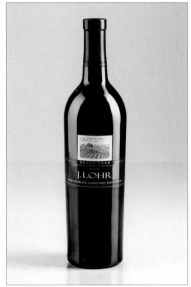

Have you ever seen a product shot of a wine bottle, or a piece of electronics, and reflected in the product you see a tall, thin, soft, rectangular reflection? Maybe even two of them? These wonderful highlight reflections are most likely from one of the mainstays of a lot of pro product shooters—a strip bank (also sometimes called a strip light). These are actually just tall, thin, rectangular softboxes (picture a softbox that's just 18" wide, but around 36" long), and they are very popular in product photography because of those wonderful tall reflections they create in products that reflect. (It's tough shooting products that are reflective, because you can see a reflection of everything in the product itself—even sometimes the photographer—so be careful when you're shooting reflective products.) You can buy strip banks for strobes, or even for the Westcott Spiderlite TD5 that I use for product photography, and the nice thing about them is that you can use them tall (vertically), or turn them on their side and use them horizontally for a really wide, wrapping light.

Using Foam Core

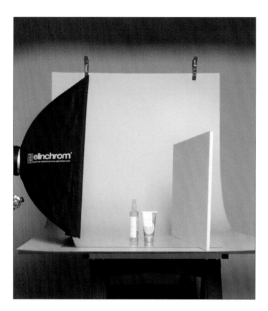 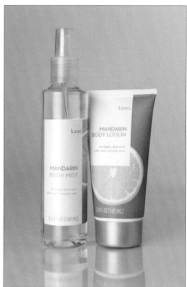

While you'll find portrait photographers using white reflectors a lot in the studio (usually to reflect or bounce light from the main light into the side of the face that's in the shadows), when it comes to product photography, more often than not, you'll find the pros using a large sheet of foam core instead. Form core tends to have a little more sheen to it than most reflectors and reflects more light. Plus, because you can cut a sheet of form core (found at most craft stores or office supply stores) down to pretty much any size you need, you can make these small enough to sit right on your product table and get right up close to your product (but just out of your viewfinder's frame).

A Dramatic Background for Products

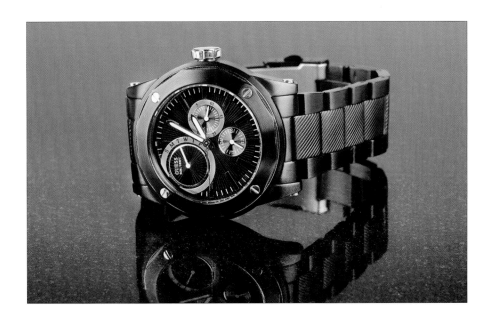

If you want to go for a dramatic look for your product shots, try this: go to your local home supply mega hardware store and buy a single tile of black granite. This stuff is incredibly reflective and just sitting your product on it makes it scream, "Shoot me!" It looks like this stuff was made for product shots, and yet it's fairly inexpensive (well, at least for one tile it is). Get as large a tile as they have in stock, but since it's unlikely to be very large, you'll use this for smaller items that you want to have a dark, dramatic look. Try this the next time you want to go a totally different direction from the standard white background that you see so often for products shots.

Use a Tripod

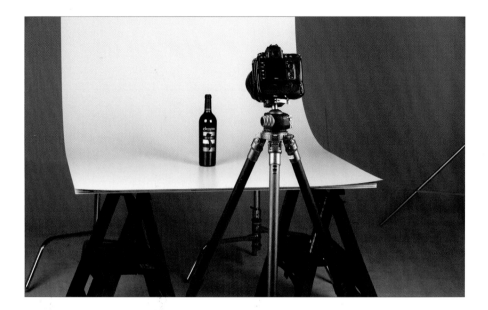

Product shots are one of those things that if they're not absolutely tack sharp, they just don't work, and that's why the pros use a tripod every time. Having that super-sharp focus is critical and, although I will hand-hold when shooting people (if I'm using studio strobes or flash to freeze any movement), when it comes to product shots, my camera goes right on a tripod and stays there. If you're looking for a way to take your product shots to the next level, this is absolutely the first step.

Hide Distracting Stuff

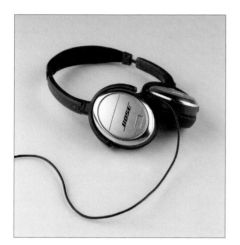 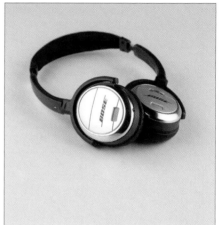

If you take a look at most professional product shots, you'll find that they go to great lengths to hide anything that would distract you from the presentation of the product, even if it's a part of the product itself. Perfect example? Headphones. You know and I know that there's a cord on headphones that plugs into our laptops, or our iPods, but in ads you rarely, if ever, see the cord—you just see the headphones (earbuds are an exception, but without the cords, they look like a couple of white peas). The photographer goes out of their way to hide things like cords, or cables, or anything else that would detract or take away from the product (like a camera strap on a camera. If you see Canons or Nikons, or, well....almost anybody's shot of their latest camera, you won't see a camera strap in the shot, even though in real life every dSLR we buy has one attached). Keep this in mind, and you'll wind up with cleaner looking shots. So, if you're shooting something with a cord that unplugs (like the headphones above), just unplug the cord and move it out of the image (as seen in the photo on the right). Otherwise, you'll have to remove the distracting object in Photoshop. I did a video for you on how to do this, and you can find it on the book's website at www.kelbytraining.com/books/digphotogv3.

Clean It Before You Shoot It

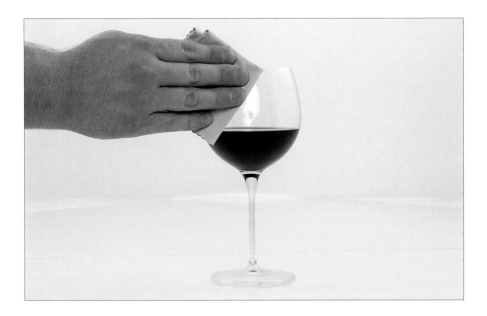

Before you shoot anything—clean it first. This is one of those things that, if you don't do it, I promise it will take you ten times longer to fix it in Photoshop than the 15 seconds it would have taken you to do it right in the studio. I can't tell you how many times in the past I've skipped this step, and I don't really notice all the fingerprints and little smudges, and specks of dust on the product until I actually open the shot later in Photoshop, and then I have to spend 10 minutes trying to retouch it all away. It's been so bad on a couple of occasions, that I actually went back, wiped down the product, and then reshot from scratch. You only have to do that a few times to learn the lesson—clean it thoroughly before you start shooting and save yourself a bunch of headaches after the shoot.

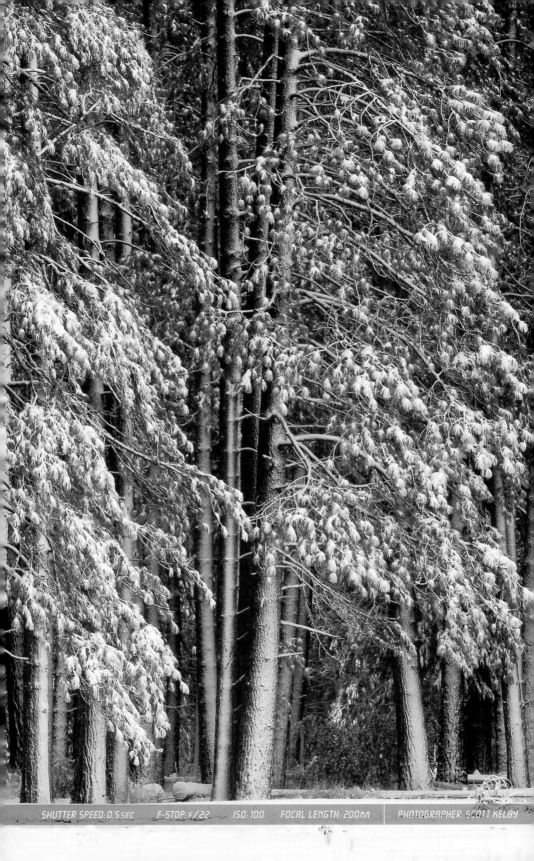

Chapter Five

Shooting Outdoors Like a Pro

More Tips for Creating Stunning Scenic Images

If you're starting to see a pattern here, it's only because there's a pattern here. That pattern is what I talked about in the brief introduction to this book, which is this book "picks up right where volume 2 left off." Okay, if that's the case, then why isn't this chapter named "Shoot Landscapes Like a Pro, Part 2" like back in Chapter 1, Part 2? That's because not all of the tips in this chapter are about shooting landscapes. (That's why, Mr. Snoop Smarty Smart!) Hey, it's not my fault—you created these questions yourself. (Did not. Did too!) Anyway, this chapter is about getting better results from shooting outdoors, and luckily for us, it's easier to get better looking images outside because so many of the problems that we run into inside (like mall security) don't exist outside. Also, light is easier to find outside. I can't tell you how many times I've been walking down the street, I look down, and there's a perfectly good flash unit just lying there on the sidewalk. Okay, that's an exaggeration (it's only happened three or four times), but since the sun is usually found outside, our job is well-defined—we have to learn ways to control the sun to our advantage. For example, if you're handy with fabric and a readily available commercial grade lathe, you'll be able to assemble a rudimentary diffusion panel that's large enough to evenly illuminate a tour bus. This comes in incredibly handy if you get a call from a tour bus company wanting you to shoot a cover shot for their new fall catalog. However, if you get a call from a florist instead, I have to be honest with you, I'm not sure how much use you're going to get out of that 23x23' frame-mounted diffusion grid, but you know what they say, that's why God invented eBay. Anyway, no matter whether you're shooting buses outside or flowers, this chapter will fully and completely avoid both of those individual topics.

Make a Packing List So You Don't Forget Anything

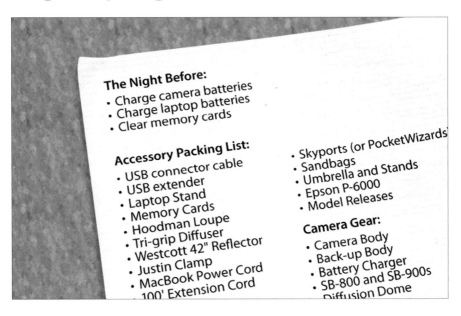

The Night Before:
- Charge camera batteries
- Charge laptop batteries
- Clear memory cards

Accessory Packing List:
- USB connector cable
- USB extender
- Laptop Stand
- Memory Cards
- Hoodman Loupe
- Tri-grip Diffuser
- Westcott 42" Reflector
- Justin Clamp
- MacBook Power Cord
- 100' Extension Cord

- Skyports (or PocketWizards)
- Sandbags
- Umbrella and Stands
- Epson P-6000
- Model Releases

Camera Gear:
- Camera Body
- Back-up Body
- Battery Charger
- SB-800 and SB-900s
- Diffusion Dome

There is nothing worse than getting out on location for a landscape shoot, or arriving in a foreign country where you hope to do some travel photography, and finding out that you forgot an important piece of gear. I've done it a dozen times. Well, at least I used to, until I started making separate gear packing lists for my landscape and travel photography trips (to see what I pack, go to Chapter 8). It doesn't have to be anything fancy, but pay particular attention to the little things you might forget, like a cleaning cloth, spare batteries, a polarizing filter, a cable release, etc. You're probably not going to forget your camera body (if you do, maybe improving your photography shouldn't be your biggest concern), so focus on those little things that you'd really miss once you're out on the shoot. One good way to do that is to mentally picture arriving on the scene, and put together your gear in your mind. At some point, you'll mentally reach into your bag for something that's not there. Add it to the list right then.

Show Movement in Your Shot

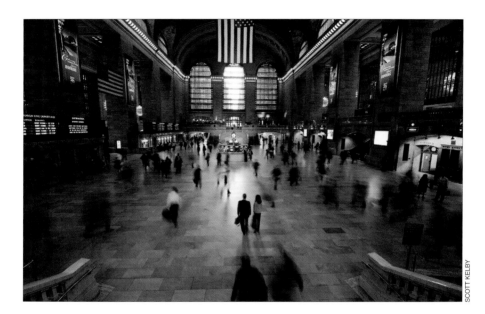

SCOTT KELBY

Showing movement is an easy way to add excitement to your photos, and it's easy to capture. The secret to showing movement is lowering your shutter speed. For example, in the shot shown above, in New York's Grand Central Station, two things have to happen for you to see the blur of people moving: (1) the station itself needs to stay sharp and crisp, so you shoot on a tripod; and (2) you use a long shutter speed, so when the shutter opens and people are walking, their movement is captured. If you're in kind of a dark setting (like the shot above), you can shoot in aperture priority mode, choose a safe all-around f-stop (like f/8), and press the shutter button. The shutter will stay open a second or two and everybody will be blurry. It's harder to get this movement effect in the middle of the day, because your shutter wants to stay open such a short time. So, what do photographers do? Probably the most popular trick is to use a screw-on darkening filter, like a neutral density filter (like those made by Singh-Ray Filters) to darken what your camera sees, so your shutter stays open longer.

Getting the Star Filter Effect

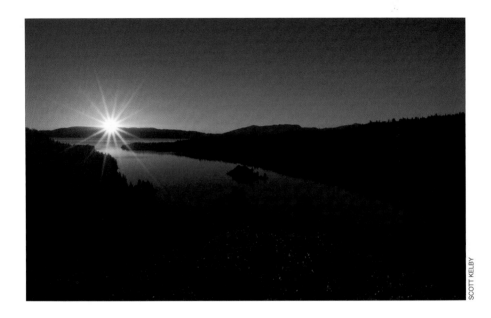

SCOTT KELBY

There are special lens filters you can buy that can turn bright lights captured in your dusk and nighttime images into starbrights. However, if you don't want to spring for the filter, you can get a similar effect right in-camera by just choosing an f-stop with the highest number you can, like f/22. This alone will usually give you that multi-point star effect without having to spend a dime.

Try Getting Creative with White Balance

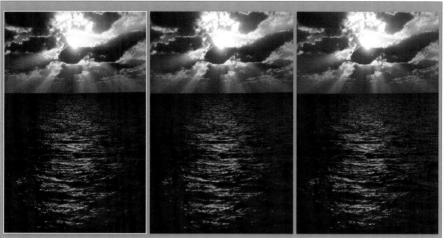

SCOTT KELBY

There are two ways to look at white balance: One is "proper" white balance, where the white balance is appropriate to the lighting situation you're shooting in. So, if you're shooting in the shade, and you've chosen a Shade setting for your white balance, your color looks normal and accurate. Then there's "creative" white balance (one of my favorites), where you choose a particular white balance because it will make the photo look the way you want it. For example, if you're up for a dawn landscape shoot, and it's a pretty flat look-ing, boring morning (lightwise), you could try changing your white balance to Tungsten, and now everything looks blue. That alone could turn a really boring daybreak into a very cool morning shoot. At dusk, changing your white balance to Shade suddenly makes everything very warm, like you had a much more exciting sunset than you did. In the example shown here, the image on the left was shot with the Auto white balance, the cen-ter one was changed to Fluorescent, and the one on the right was set to Tungsten. These aren't accurate white balances, they are you being creative in the camera by making the scene cooler (more blue) or warmer (more yellow) because regular white balance, while accurate, looks so…I dunno…regular. Give it a try the next time you're on location and the light doesn't cooperate.

Let Great Light Be Your Subject

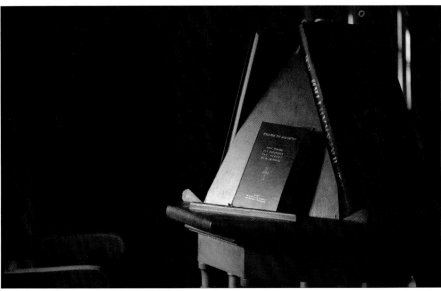

SCOTT KELBY

Every once in a while, you get an amazing subject in front of you, and there just happens to be beautiful, amazing light on it. The problem is that this only happens every once in a while. However, beautiful light happens all around us, so instead of waiting for your subject to be bathed in beautiful light, start looking for beautiful light, and then once you find it, start looking for a subject that's in and around that light. Places I look for beautiful light are usually places with natural light, so when traveling, keep an eye out for great light in places like markets, little alleyways, old abandoned buildings, workshops, small churches, anywhere with skylights, or any building with really dirty windows (which create soft, diffused light). Outside, you can find great light around sunrise or sunset, but beyond that, keep an eye out for great light right after a rain storm. Sometimes, where the sun breaks through the clouds, you can have beautiful light appear, even if it's just for a few minutes. In short, when you come across some beautiful light, start looking for a subject, because just about whatever you shoot in it is going to be beautiful.

Watch for Bright Spots

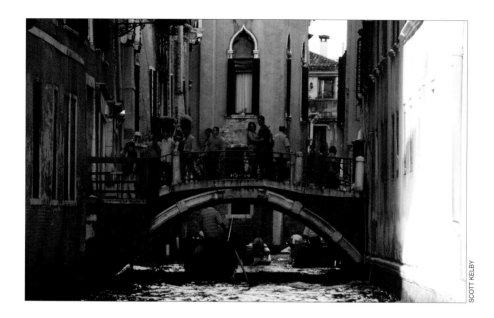

SCOTT KELBY

If you're on vacation shooting friends, family, or locals, keep this in mind: avoid taking shots where something bright is near your subject (a bright beam of sunlight, or an area lit brightly by the sun, while your subject is in the shade, etc.). By nature, the eye is drawn immediately to that bright spot first, not to your subject (in the image shown here, the bright wall on the right side of the image draws your eye away from the subjects on the bridge). So, when you see a bright area near your subject, change the position you're shooting from (move left or right) and compose that bright area right out of your shot.

Compose to Hide Modern-Day Objects

If you're shooting a travel photo, and you really want to emphasize the charm of the scene, try to compose the shot so you don't see modern day objects. For example, nothing kills that charming shot of the boat in the misty harbor like a 250-horsepower Evinrude motor hanging off the back. Look for a boat in the harbor that looks timeless, and try to exclude other boats around it that have modern looking engines, or radar dishes, or other modern day accessories to capture that charming look. Same thing in the city—exclude the new pay phone, mailbox, garbage can, posters, etc.

The Three Keys to Landscape Photography

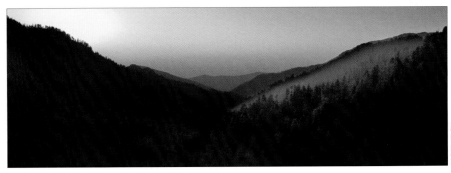

SCOTT KELBY

Successful landscape photography is made up of three things: (1) having the right equipment and knowing how to use it, (2) doing your homework and scouting your locations in advance, so when the light is great, you're in the right place at the right time, and (3) sheer unadulterated luck. Sadly, #3 plays a bigger role than you'd think, and here's why: You get up crazy early and get out to your location. You get your gear set up, and it's all ready to go. You know your equipment inside and out, and you're comfortable with your exposure, composition, and the whole nine yards. Then it starts pouring rain. Or a thick fog rolls in. Or it's perfectly clear, and it's just a blah sunrise with no clouds in the sky—it wasn't a majestic morning, it was dark one minute and then, a few minutes later, it got bright. Blah. It happens all the time. You're at the mercy of Mother Nature and dumb luck. It's a total roll of the dice whether you're going to get a spectacular sunrise or a murky mess, but you can tilt the odds in your favor big time by following one simple rule: return to that same location more than once. That's right, if you know it's a great location, and you were there on a blah morning, go back the next morning, and the next. If you're persistent, you're going to be there one morning when the light is just magical, the cloud pattern is just right, and you see colors you didn't know existed. You'll be there when the water in the lake is like glass, and the dawn light couldn't be more stunning. I've been on location on a few dawn shoots just like that. But just a few. More often than not, it's blah. So what do I do? I go back. The more I go back, the greater my chances are that I'll be there on a morning I'll talk about for years.

Look for Clouds to Hold the Color

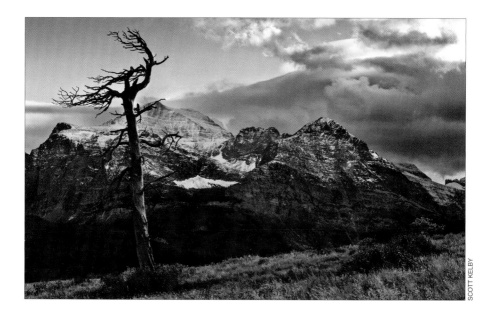

SCOTT KELBY

When it comes to shooting landscapes at sunrise or sunset, clouds are usually your friends. Not a blanket of clouds, mind you, but scattered clouds. The reason is you need something to hold the color in the sky. You need something for nature's gradients of color, that happen right around sunset, to play off of, and that something is clouds. If you've ever witnessed an empty, cloudless sky at sunset or sunrise, you know how lifeless they can be, so don't let a weather report that's calling for clouds the next day scare you off from your shoot. Sometimes, it's those clouds that turn the ordinary into the extraordinary.

Shoot Shadows

In the studio, we try to manage shadows—make them softer, smoother, or we even make them disappear altogether—but outside the studio, the shadows themselves make great subjects. So, make the shadows the subject—long shadows, hard shadows, distorted shadows. You can also let intentional shadows add to your location shots by putting objects between the light and a wall behind or beside your subject. This popular trick can add a lot of interest when you're shooting a blank, empty wall.

How to Shoot Underwater, Part 1

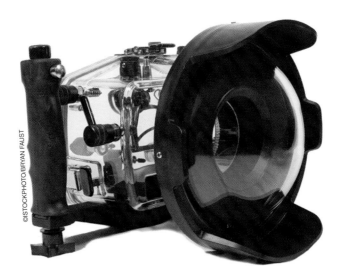

©ISTOCKPHOTO/BRYAN FAUST

If you're a travel photographer, you're probably doing a lot of your photography while you're on vacation, and if you're on vacation in a tropical place, at some point you're going to go snorkeling or diving, and at that point you'll be wondering, "How can I get shots of this coral reef?" It's easier than you'd think, but there are two parts to the equation: The first part is getting a waterproof housing for your camera, but before we go any further, when I say "your camera," I mean that small point-and-shoot camera that you also take with you when you're on vacation. The reason I say this is that underwater housings for dSLR cameras (shown here) often cost more than the camera (with a good lens) itself. I'm not exaggerating—it's amazing what they cost. So, unless you plan on making a career of underwater photography, take your point-and-shoot, and buy an underwater housing for somewhere around $150. In fact, it would be much, much cheaper for you to buy a brand new high-end point-and-shoot (like the excellent Canon G10) and an underwater housing for it, than it would to buy just about any housing for your existing dSLR. I can't explain it, but sadly, that's the way it is. So, the first part of this is to buy your housing, and resign yourself to the fact that you're not taking your dSLR underwater, unless you're just incredibly loose with money. Part 2 is on the next page.

How to Shoot Underwater, Part 2

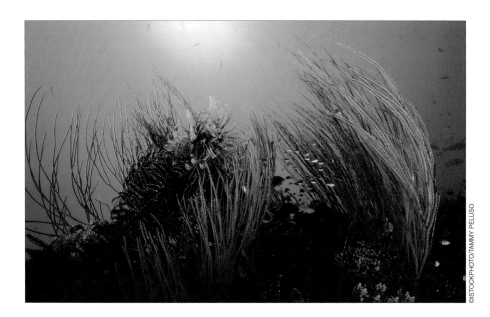

©ISTOCKPHOTO/TAMMY PELUSO

Once you've got your underwater housing, there are a couple of challenges you're go-ing to face. First, there are things underwater that want to eat you. But that aside, one of your biggest issues will be light, or really the lack thereof. Ideally, when shooting in deeper water, having a flash or other light source is the only way to get good color in your photo. If you're shooting near the surface, you'll probably be able to keep a fairly low ISO, but once you start going down 30–40 feet, take a look at your shutter speed and you'll shudder (sorry, that was lame). The light down at this depth is low, and if you start getting shutter speeds of 1/30, 1/15, or below, what you're going to get is a bunch of in-credibly blurry photos, but sadly, you won't know that until they're on your computer (or you've made prints), because (say it with me now, everybody) everything looks in focus on your tiny LCD screen. So, if you're buying a point-and-shoot for underwater photog-raphy, try to find one that has fairly low noise at higher ISO. Your other problem is going to be color casts, and a general murkiness or haze over your photos. The good news is that Photoshop can usually fix this automatically. I'm not a big fan of "Auto" settings in Photoshop, but this is one case where it works surprisingly well. Go under Photoshop's (or Photoshop Elements') Image menu, under Adjustments, and choose Auto Levels. That alone will usually do the trick.

It's What You Leave Out of the Frame

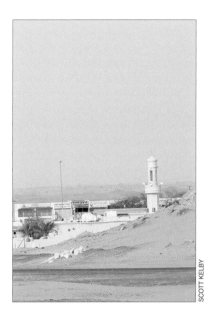
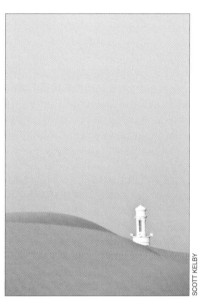

SCOTT KELBY

SCOTT KELBY

I learned a great lesson one day from talking with David duChemin, a gifted travel and editorial photographer. I was in love with a photo he had taken of an old man sweeping inside an entryway, right in front of the Taj Mahal. It seemed like it must have been taken at dawn, because there was literally no one there but him, so I asked David how he got so lucky to be there when virtually no one else was there. He told me that actually there were tourists everywhere, and if he had shot a little wider I would have seen hundreds of people on either side of him. What he had done was make a conscious decision about what to leave out of his shot. He framed the shot so just that one man was in his frame, and it made it look like he and that man were the only two people there that day. In the example here, these two shots were taken seconds apart and the only difference is the framing. The shot on the left was taken from a standing position and you could see the gift shop, road, and other distracting stuff. Now, all I had to do to hide that stuff was kneel down behind the small sand dune in front of me and frame the shot so that only the tower was visible. The lesson: It's not always what you put in your frame—it's sometimes what you leave out.

Shoot the Reflections in Puddles

Here's another creative idea: shoot the reflections you find in puddles. I don't mean shoot a downtown with puddles in the foreground where you see a reflection, I mean shoot the puddles themselves. If you're in a city, there's something reflecting in those puddles—find the angle that looks best, and shoot it. Ya never know what you'll come up with.

Shoot at the Lowest ISO Possible

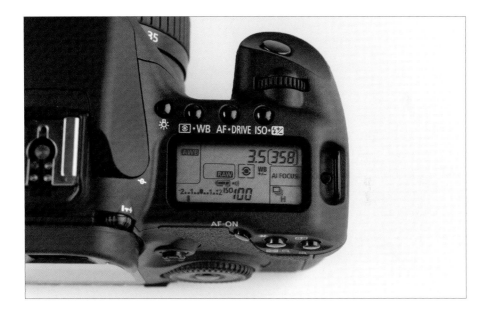

If you're shooting landscapes, you're probably shooting at around dusk and around dawn, and if that's the case, you're probably shooting on a tripod, and if that's the case (see how I'm stringing this whole case together?), then you need to be shooting at the lowest ISO your camera will allow (usually ISO 200 on most Nikon dSLRs, or ISO 100 on Canons). The reason why is you'll get the sharpest, most noise-free, best quality images at your lowest ISO, and because you're on a tripod, you don't need to raise your ISO above that sweet spot (remember, raising your ISO is usually for hand-holding in low light; you're not hand-holding, you're on a tripod, so go for the ultimate in quality).

The Noise You See Onscreen Sometimes Goes Away

If you shot at 400 or 800 ISO, chances are when you open that photo on your computer, you're going to see some noise (depending on how well your camera handles noise, you'll either see a little or a lot), but don't let that throw you—even though you see some noise onscreen, a lot of times that noise will disappear when you actually print the image.

Not Sure What to Shoot? Try This!

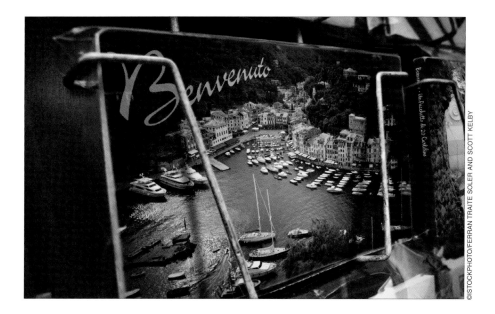

If you've ever arrived in a city while on vacation and you don't have any idea where or what to shoot, your first stop should be a local gift shop to look at their postcards. If you see any interesting locations, it will usually tell you the name of them on the back of the postcard, or you can show the postcard to the shopkeeper and ask them where it's located. Okay, so why not just buy the postcard and head for the bar? Because we're photographers, that's why. Plus, we might be able to come back with some better images than the ones on the postcards they're selling (in fact, maybe next year they'll be selling your shots as their postcards, and hopefully, they're doing so with your permission and a commission).

Shoot Texture as Your Subject

A very popular subject to shoot, especially for travel photographers, is texture—anything from flaking paint on the wall of an old building, to the grain on the wood table at a café. Texture is everywhere, and can have great dimension if the light hitting it is from the side, because side lighting will enhance the texture as the shadows add interest and depth. Keep an eye out for texture when you're roaming city streets.

Keeping Unwanted Light Out

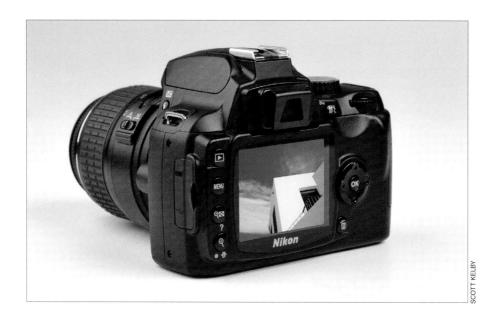

SCOTT KELBY

Here's a great tip I picked up, from renown wildlife and outdoor photographer Moose Peterson, for getting better exposure in your landscape photos when you're using a cable release to fire your camera (you use a cable release to minimize any camera shake that's caused by your finger pressing the shutter button). The problem is this: since you're using a cable release, your eye isn't right up to the viewfinder like it normally would be, so you're not blocking the light from coming in through the viewfinder and messing with your exposure. The solution is to cover your viewfinder. Some cameras, like Nikon's D3 and D3x, have a built-in viewfinder door you can close—the switch is to the left of the eyepiece itself—but most other Nikon dSLRs come with the DK-5 eyepiece cap (shown above) that snaps into place to keep light out of your viewfinder in cases like this. By the way, you can test to see if light is getting in through the viewfinder and affecting your exposure by covering and uncovering the viewfinder with your hand. If you see the shutter speed change at all, then light is getting in. If you don't have that little door, Moose recommends hanging your lens cap over the viewfinder to block the light. If you're a Canon shooter, most Canon dSLRs come with an eyepiece cover that covers the viewfinder and keeps outside light from affecting your exposure.

Using a Graduated Neutral Density Filter

If the polarizing filter is the most important filter for landscape photographers, then a graduated neutral density filter has to be the second most important. This filter is designed to help you do something your camera can't usually do on its own, and that is expose for the foreground without overexposing the sky. That's why this filter has become so popular—it darkens the sky, but it's how it does it that really creates a pleasing effect. This filter is graduated, so it's darkest at the top of the sky, and then it graduates down to full transparency (like a gradient), so the ground doesn't get darkened at all. The one I use is actually rectangular plastic, and I simply hold it up in front of my lens then take the shot. I don't use a lot of filters, in fact just a few (go to Chapter 3 to see the other ones I use), but this is one that makes a really big difference, and that's why it's with me on every landscape shoot.

Get Down Low

We shoot pretty much everything from a standing position. So, everything looks just like it would to anyone walking by that same spot. Try something from a different perspective—a view people wouldn't normally see. Get down low—really, really low. If you go down on one knee, you see things from a young child's perspective. Sit on the floor, and you've got a toddler's point of view. But if you really want to take it to the next level, lie on the floor and shoot, showing a perspective normally seen by squirrels (it gives you some idea why they're so nervous all the time).

How to Shoot for HDR

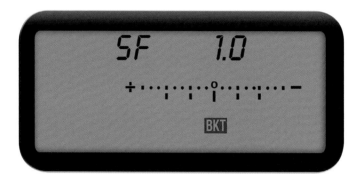

If you want to create HDR (High Dynamic Range) images (where you shoot multiple images, then combine and tone map them into a single image with a range of tones beyond
what your camera alone can capture), here are some tips to make the shooting part easier.
The first tip for HDR success is to shoot with your camera on a tripod (your software tweaking later will be a lot easier). Next, you'll need to set up your camera to shoot in aperture
priority mode, then set your camera to take automatic bracketed exposures. Here's how:

Nikon: Press-and-hold the function (Fn) button on the bottom front of your camera (if
you have a D300, D700, D3, or D3x), then move the main command dial on the back of
your camera until you see bracketing turned on in your top LCD. Choose five bracketed
shots (so it takes one regular exposure, then one brighter, one way brighter, one darker,
and one way darker). Now switch your camera to continuous high-speed release mode,
then hold down the shutter button until your camera takes all five shots for you.

Canon: Press-and-hold the Mode and AF•Drive buttons to turn on auto exposure
bracketing (set the number of shots to 5 in the Custom Functions menu, so it takes one
regular exposure, then one brighter, one way brighter, one darker, and one way darker).
Now switch your camera to shoot in burst mode, then hold down the shutter button
until your camera takes all five shots for you.

What to Do with Your HDR Shots

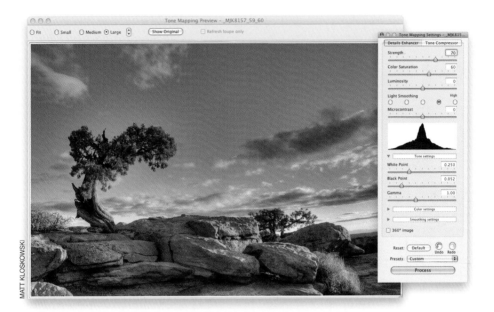

MATT KLOSKOWSKI

Shooting the bracketed shots is only one part of the equation, because all you've got is five shots, and four of them are either overexposed or underexposed. So, what you need now is a program to combine these into a single HDR image, which is what our goal is. The program that's the most widely used is called Photomatix Pro (from HDRsoft.com), and it runs $99. You can also download a fully working demo version for a Mac or PC (the trial never expires, but it does apply a watermark to your images). You open your five images in Photomatix Pro, and it does all the combining and tone mapping for you. I recorded a video tutorial just for you to show you how to use Photomatix Pro to create your first HDR image, and you can find it at www.kelbytraining.com/books/digphotogv3.

Scout Your Dawn Shoot Location

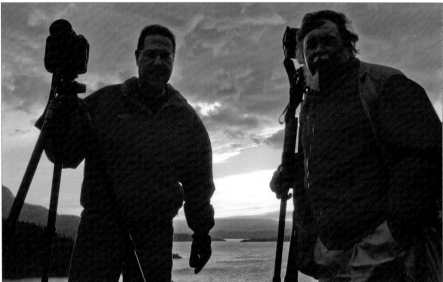

BARNEY STREIT

I'll never forget the first time I shot at Big Sur, along California's coast near Monterey and Carmel, a number of years ago. It was a mess. I had been in town earlier that day, but didn't think to go scout out a good shooting location, and the next morning, well before dawn, we headed out to the coast, where we found ourselves driving around in the dark trying to figure out where a good place to shoot was, but of course, we couldn't see any-thing—it was pitch black. Out of desperation, we pulled off at a "scenic" overlook (well, that's what the sign said anyway), and we set up our gear, waiting for sunrise, and then as the sun came up, I proceeded to capture some of the most unremarkable, bland, and forgettable images ever taken of Big Sur. In the dark, not surprisingly, we picked a totally blah spot. If I had done my homework and scouted a location, I would have at least had a shot of something really special. A lesson learned. Since then, I go out of my way to find a great shooting location first, and if I can, I take a test shot, even if it's during terrible light. That way, if the shot looks decent in bad light, all I have to do is come back and try for that same shot in great light. It's a recipe for success, and this little bit of homework up front will put you in the best position for something magical to happen.

Don't Always Shoot Wide Angle

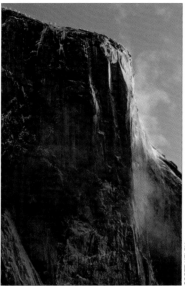

SCOTT KELBY

If you're into shooting landscapes, you're into shooting wide angle, and that totally makes sense, because most landscape photographers want to take in as much of a beautiful, sweeping landscape as possible. But the next time you're out in the field, try something different—take out a long telephoto lens and capture a totally different side of your location. Sometimes you can uncover amazing photo opportunities that are just outside the reach of your wide-angle lens. It lets you bring a totally different perspective to your landscape photography, and opens the door to a new way of shooting outdoors that you just might fall in love with. Give it a try the next time you're out shooting—you might be surprised at what's waiting just 100mm or so away.

Shoot Shapes (Circles, Squares)

I got this idea from my buddy and commercial photographer Joe Glyda, who gives himself specific shooting assignments for a specific amount of time. For example, he'll give himself a one-hour assignment in a downtown area to shoot nothing but things that are round. Or square. I'm constantly amazed at what he comes up with, and you'll be amazed at how a well-defined assignment like this will bring out your creativity. Just remember, no cheating—you have to give yourself the assignment before you arrive at the shooting locale.

Use Backlighting to Your Advantage

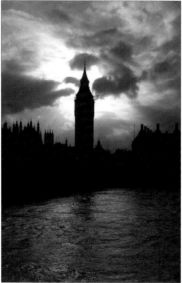

SCOTT KELBY

Although we often avoid backlighting when shooting travel portraits (unless we have a fill flash, of course), when it comes to shooting landscape photography, you can get some amazingly dramatic images when the sunlight is aiming right at you (rather than over your shoulder). You can even sometimes compose the shot with the sun right in the shot itself, and if you're shooting at a high f-stop number (like f/22), the sun will even get little light flares and starbursts that can look really captivating. Now, because you're shooting right into the sun, it can be a little trickier to come away with a killer shot, so don't be disappointed if, the first time out, you don't come home with something to frame for your wall. It takes a bit of practice—trial and error—to find the right exposure, and how to frame the shot so the sun actually isn't in every photo (just the backlighting effect), but believe me, when you nail it, you'll know.

Why We Get There Early

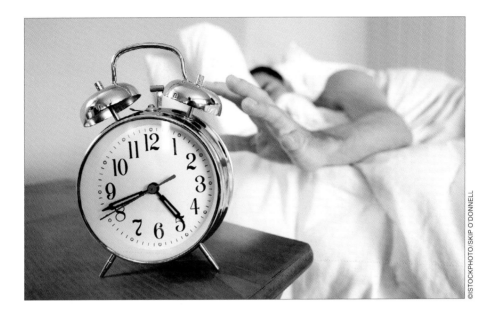

©ISTOCKPHOTO/SKIP O'DONNELL

As I mentioned in volume 1, the two best times of the day to shoot landscapes are dawn and dusk, and if you choose to shoot at either one of these (and I hope you do), make sure you get to your shooting location plenty early. Earlier than you'd think. I can't tell you how many times I've seen photographers scrambling to get their gear out of the car, then they lug all their stuff out to the location, huffing and puffing, and all the while, those few minutes of incredible light are nearly gone, and you've never seen more stressed out, frustrated, and downright angry photographers than when that happens. Look, if you're getting up at 5:00 a.m. to catch sunrise nearby, instead get up at 4:45 a.m. and be on location, all set up, ready, composed, and relaxed, so you can not only get the shot, but you can enjoy the experience, too.

Shooting a Popular Landscape Destination? The Good Spots Go First!

If you're heading out to shoot a popular landscape destination, like the Arches National Park in Utah, keep in mind that the shooting locations you hike out to fill up very fast. So fast, that if you don't get there two hours before dawn, you might not get a place to set up your tripod at all. If you do get a spot, it may be behind 50 other photographers. These prime locations just don't have enough space, and the ideal shooting spot can sometimes only accommodate a handful of photographers, so if you plan a trip to shoot there, also plan to get there crazy early and be one of those handful with the ideal shooting position.

Why You Should Shoot Panos Vertically

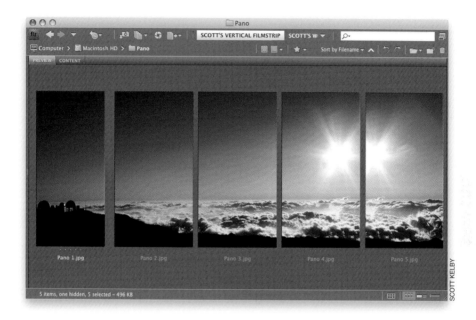

If you have Photoshop (at least version CS3 or higher), you absolutely should be shoot-ing panoramas, because Photoshop will automatically stitch your individual images into a wide (or tall) panoramic image for you, and it does an absolutely amazing job. These days, you don't even have to pull a bunch of fancy tricks in the camera (you can even hand-hold your panos), you just have to follow one simple rule: make sure each photo overlaps by around 20%. Photoshop needs that overlap to do its thing. However, here's a tip that will keep you from having to crop off mountaintops or crop away something interesting in the foreground. Once Photoshop creates your pano, you'll always have to crop the photo a little bit because of the way it assembles your pano. Now, here's the tip: shoot your panos vertically. That way, when you crop your photo, you won't have to shear off the tip of a mountain, or part of a beautiful reflecting lake, because there will be a little "breathing room" left above your mountain range to crop in and still keep your mountains intact. Of course, if you compose so there's 1/16 of an inch above the tallest peak, the shooting vertical thing won't help, so I guess it's really two tips: shoot your pa-nos in vertical orientation, and compositionally, leave a little breathing room above your subject in case you have to crop.

Getting More Vibrant Landscapes

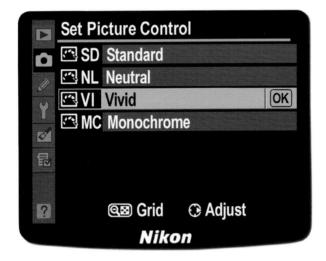

For years, traditional film photographers who shot landscapes used to be hooked on a brand of Fuji film called Velvia, because that film had a very vibrant, color-saturated look that landscape photographers just love. So much so that some simply wouldn't shoot without it. Today, with many digital cameras, we have something similar (which makes your images look more vibrant) right in the camera, but you can only take advantage of it if you're shooting in JPEG format. Nikon calls these "picture controls" and Canon calls them "picture styles," but they both do a similar thing: make your colors more vibrant. Here's how to turn this on:

Nikon: Go to the Shooting menu, and choose Set Picture Control. In the Set Picture Control menu, choose Vivid, then select OK to give you more vivid landscape photos when shooting in JPEG.

Canon: Go to the menus, to the Shooting menu, and choose Picture Style. Then choose Landscape to give you more vivid landscape photos when shooting in JPEG.

Delete Now Instead of Later

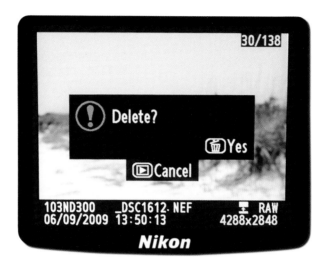

When I'm shooting travel photography, I make it a point to edit as I go—if I take a shot and see that it's blurry, or way overexposed, or just messed up in general, I delete it right there on the spot (after all, if I can see it's blurry or really bad on that tiny screen on the back of my camera, when I see it at full size it will be beyond unusable). There's no sense in carrying around these shots, which are just taking up space on your memory card, and soon they'll be just taking up space on your computer, when either way, they're destined to be deleted. So, why not save time, save space, and up the number of "keepers" from your shoot by deleting the obviously bad shots now? I usually do this in between shoots, so if I stop at a café for a snack, I'll take a look through the images I've captured, and delete the obviously really bad shots. There are some people who are hesitant to do this, because they're afraid that some blurry, overexposed shot is going to be "the one!" That's certainly never happened to me. I've seen shots that would have been great if they hadn't been blurry, or soft, or improperly exposed, but I've never used one of those for anything. You won't either. It'll just make you sigh and think, "Man, if that had only been in focus!"

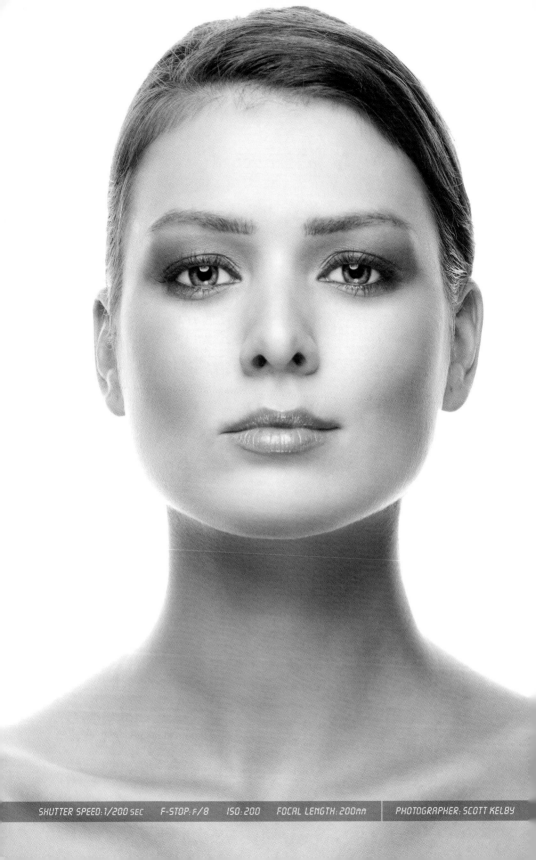

Chapter Six

Shooting People
Like a Pro

Yet Even More Tips to Make
People Look Their Very Best

How can there possibly be yet even more tips about how to make people look their very best? It's easy: have you ever looked at people? I mean, really looked at them. Up close. It's scary. I'm not talking about me or you, mind you. Other people. Let's take your average guy, for example. If he's above the age of 12 or so, most likely he has hair coming out of his nose, his ears, his underarms, and it's growing like ivy on his arms, legs—just about anywhere you wouldn't actually want hair growing. These are just the places you can see. I know. Gross. Anyway, what are we, as photographers, to do about shooting these grotesque human fur balls? We find ways to light them, using either natural light, studio light, or some twisted combination of the two, so that they're somewhat bearable to look at, as long we don't look very closely. This applies to all men, with the possible exception of George Clooney. Now, when I look at George Clooney, I see kind of a well-groomed, decent looking guy, but the women I know, including those who are photographers, see something entirely different in him. They don't see the hairy mass I described previously. They have the same reaction to him that they have to chocolate cake. They lose complete control of their faculties. So, based on this (my conclusions are strictly based on my own personal observations, and not scientific data, though I've never met a female scientist that didn't find George Clooney irresistible in a chocolate-molten-lava-cake kind of way), I decided to conduct an experiment. I went to my local bakery, had the woman who owns the bakery choose the hands-down yummiest chocolate cake she sells, and then I used a series of A-clamps and gaffer's tape to affix this to the head of my assistant Brad to see if this would bring about the "Clooney reaction," despite his having no Clooney-like resemblance. Well, it worked better than I had expected, and within two weeks he wound up marrying a supermodel from Prague, who to this day refers to herself as Mrs. Clooney. True story.

If They Look Uncomfortable,
Hand Them a Prop

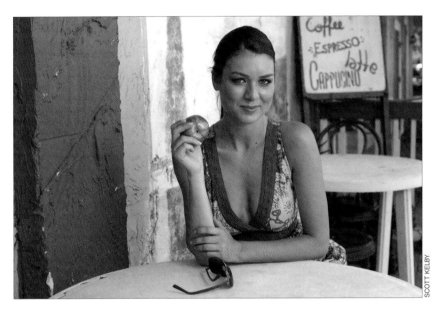

SCOTT KELBY

One of the things that makes some people so uncomfortable in front of the camera is that they don't know what to do with their hands—no matter what they do with them, they feel like they look dumb. If you can see that's the case with one of your subjects, give them something to hold (like a prop), and you'll instantly see their comfort level go up, and that will translate into more natural-looking photos. If you can give them a prop that they can relate to, all the better. (For example, if they're an artist, have them pick up a handful of paintbrushes. Shooting a nutritionist? Have her take a bite of an apple. Okay, it doesn't have to be quite as obvious as that, but you get the idea.) Once they have something in their hands they feel comfortable with, not only will they feel more comfortable, but your photos will have added visual interest, as well.

The Advantage of Having Your Subject Sit

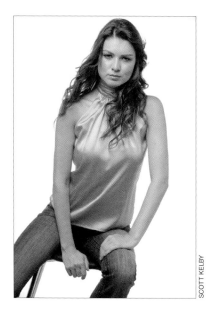

SCOTT KELBY

Another situation where your subject will often feel awkward or uncomfortable is when they're standing. They feel so vulnerable just standing there alone in an empty space, and that's why some photographers choose to have their subjects sit down. Although you'll have to shoot from a lower position (which might make you a little uncomfortable), most people will be much more comfortable sitting vs. standing. Also, if you see your subject is still really uncomfortable, try putting a small table (like a posing table, for example) in front of them. Putting something in front of them like that will help them feel less vulnerable (think of how often public speakers like to hide behind a podium when giving their presentation—it's a comfort thing). Next time you're in one of those situations where you can tell your subject feels really awkward, have 'em take a seat and you'll usually see a world of difference.

Use a Posing Stool

You can have your subject sit on just a regular ol' chair, but if you want a chair specifically for photography (one without a back or arms), you can buy a posing stool, which is an adjustable-height stool that swivels, and they're pretty unobtrusive (which is good, as its job is to not draw attention to itself, and keep the focus on the subject). You can also buy an adjustable-height posing table, as well (B&H Photo sells them separately, or you can buy them together in a kit).

Shoot From Up Really High

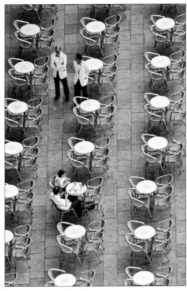

SCOTT KELBY

Another perspective we don't get to see very often is a very high perspective, and by that I mean shooting down from a second floor walkway or shooting straight down on boats going under a bridge. These high vantage points offer a view we don't see every day (even though we may walk across a second floor walkway that's open to the lower level, we don't often see images taken from that vantage point). These work great for everything from shooting the bride encircled by her bridesmaids to shooting down on diners at an outdoor cafe. The shot above was taken straight down from my hotel room window while on vacation. Next time you want a totally different perspective on things, and don't feel like getting your pants dirty from sitting down, look up and see if there's a higher angle you could be shooting from.

Have Them Get a Leg Up!

Having your subject prop one of their legs up on a box does two things: (1) it helps their overall lines, improving their overall look, and (2) it usually makes them feel a little more comfortable (now that they're not just standing there). Many photographers use this trick whether their subject is sitting or standing. It doesn't have to be a very high box (in fact, it shouldn't be); it can just be six or eight inches tall—enough to give your subject that little extra something.

Shooting a ¾-View? Pick a Spot to Look At

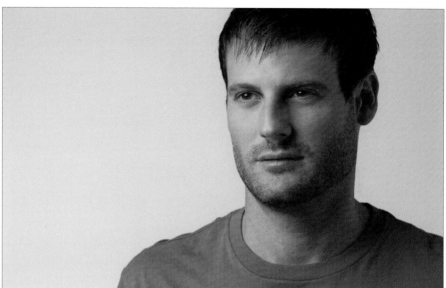

SCOTT KELBY

One of the three most popular positions for formal portraits is the ¾-view, which shows about three-quarters of your subject's face—they're looking away from the camera at around a 45° angle (as if they're looking at something off to the side of where the photographer is standing, and because their head is turned slightly like this, you see both eyes, but you don't see the ear on the other side of their head). But this tip isn't how to pose a ¾-view, it's about how to get a more realistic-looking ¾-view without seeing too much of the whites of your subject's eye (if you get too much of the whites of the eyes, it looks kind of weird. Okay, it looks kind of creepy). The trick is: don't just have your subject look off to the left or right—choose a particular object in the room that they should focus on each time they do the ¾-view. Once you give your subject a spot to look at, take a test shot and see if you can see their irises clearly and there's not too much of the whites of the eyes showing. If you do see lots of white, they're looking too far away—have them turn their head a little more toward the camera and focus on a different object in the room (if there's nothing for them to focus on, put an extra light stand where you want them to look, and raise the top of the stand to where you want their eyes to go). Also, this picking-a-spot-for-the-¾-view technique is particularly helpful when working with professional models, because they'll be hitting a number of different poses during the shoot. If you give them a spot to look at each time they go for that ¾-view, they'll hit that same spot every time.

Get Everything Set Before They Arrive

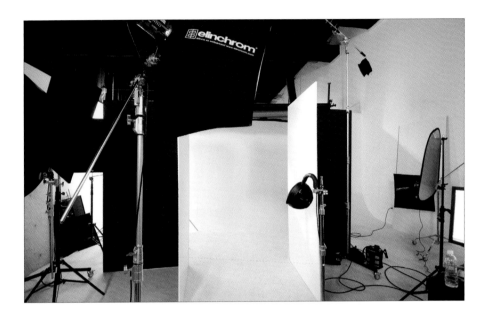

If you're doing a studio shoot, you want to keep your subject as comfortable and relaxed as possible, and one way to do that is to not keep them waiting around—have everything set up, tested, and ready when they get there. You shouldn't be in the middle of setting up the lights, or adjusting your camera gear, or anything else when your subject arrives for the shoot. Have everything ready (test all the lighting—not only to make sure it works, but have it set up approximately where you want it, and have your exposure pretty well set) when they walk in the door. Don't have your subject sitting there for 20 minutes while you try to get the lighting right, or while you're trying to get your camera settings right. Besides looking unprofessional to your subject, they're going to be uncomfortable sitting there and not posing while you're testing everything (I have a subject who can't help but smile and pose, even when I'm just testing the lights, and then when it's time to actually start smiling, they've been doing it for 20 minutes already—they're "smiled out"). So, to increase your chances of success, to keep your subject relaxed, and to conduct your shoot like a pro, have everything ready when they walk in the door.

Super-Shallow Depth of Field for Portraits

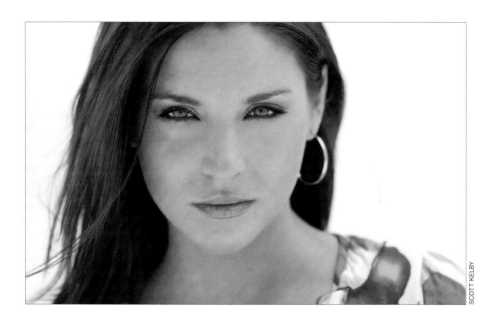

SCOTT KELBY

Right now, one of the most popular looks for casual and location portraits is to use a very, very shallow depth of field, so everything is pretty much way out of focus except your subject. You get this look in two steps: (1) You have to have a lens that will allow you to shoot at a very low-numbered f-stop (like f/1.8 or f/1.4), so most folks use a fixed focal length lens (like a 50mm lens—it's not a zoom lens, it just shoots at a fixed length of 50mm, but that's okay, that's the depth we're going for), because they're not too terribly expensive (usually less than $100). And, (2) for a location portrait, to be able to shoot outdoors at such a wide-open f-stop, you have to shoot when it's really overcast, you're totally in dark shade (like in an alley), or it's nearly sunset. If not, shooting at that low of an f-stop number will totally overexpose your photos, and they'll be so bright they'll be unusable. So, pull this technique out of your bag on those cloudy, overcast, gray days—go to a downtown location, and do your best to compose so you don't see the sky. Also, make sure you're careful about your focus, because if you're off by even a little, they'll be out of focus. Focus directly on your subject's eyes, and understand that everything behind their eyes (like the back of their head or their earrings, as in the shot above) will either be a little, or a lot, out of focus.

Using a Triflector for Portraits

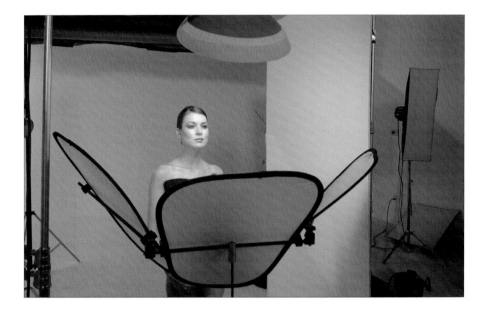

Another handy piece of gear for shooting fashion and beauty style portraits is a triflector, and what this is, is three small reflectors that mount on one thin horizontal bar. They're hinged so you can aim them right where you want them and create some amazing wraparound light (well, reflected light—they're reflecting light from a light positioned above your subject). Because you have three of these aimable reflectors, you can not only just reflect light on the center of your subject's face, you can aim the side reflectors up to put reflected light onto the sides of your subject's face, giving you a bright, clean look (which is why these have become so popular with beauty and fashion photographers). Another nice bonus of using these triflectors is the great catch lights they create in your subject's eyes. There are a number of companies that now make these and I've tried a few different ones, but the one I regularly use is the Trilite from Lastolite, with silver reflectors on one side and white on the other (I like how light-weight it is, and how easy it is to set up, but it doesn't feel cheap and chintzy).

Using Scrims for Shooting in Direct Sun

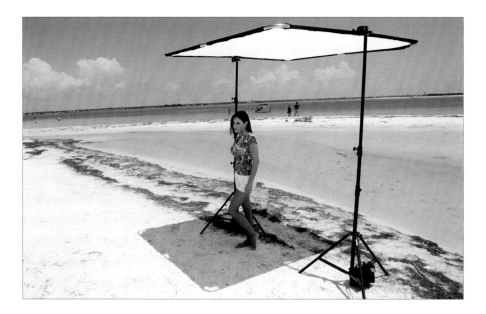

If you've ever wondered how the pros get those amazing portraits out in direct sunlight, like at the beach, or out in the middle of the day in a field, here's the trick: they don't. They're not shooting in direct daylight, because what you can't see, just outside the frame, is a large scrim positioned a few feet above the subject that diffuses and softens the light. Think of it kind of like a giant softbox that spreads the light from the sun. What's nice about scrims is they're very lightweight and portable (it's just fabric wrapped around, or attached to, a collapsible frame), and they're not crazy expensive (you can get a pretty decent-sized one, like 78x78" with frame and fabric, for around $375). Once you get your scrim, you're going to need to have a way to support it, because it has to go between the sun and your subject (they're usually put either directly over your subject, like a roof, or behind or beside them at a 45° angle). These are really lightweight, so you can have an assistant (or a couple of friends) support your scrim frame, or you can support them with light stands. If you go the stand route, you'll need to buy two little brackets that fit on top of your light stands to hold and tilt the frame, so don't forget to get those, too. Also, you'll probably want to bring a reflector, and maybe even a flash, depending on how late in the day you'll be shooting.

Shooting at the Beach

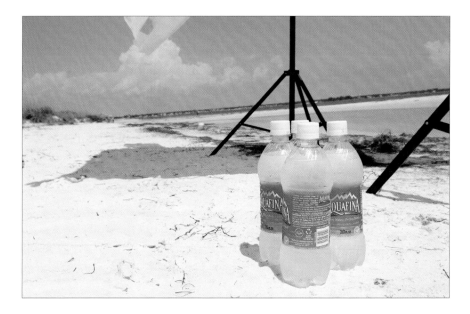

Besides just shooting in a really bright, direct sun environment (see the previous page for dealing with that), shooting at the beach presents its own set of challenges that you'll want to consider before doing a beach shoot. The first is sand—the natural enemy of camera gear. It doesn't take much wind for that fine sand to start blowing around, so if you're out on location and need to change your lens, your best bet is to go back to your car and change lenses there, or bring a changing bag that you can stick your camera body and lenses inside of to do the quick switch-a-roo. Also, once your shoot is done and you're back in the studio, don't forget to clean the outside of your camera and your lenses, especially if you were shooting near salt water. Outside of that, don't forget to bring the non-camera things like bottled water for everyone on the shoot, a fresh change of clothes (and towels) if you're going to be shooting in the water at all, and (I know this probably goes without saying, but I'm going to say it anyway) bring sun-screen and reapply it often.

Shooting on the Street

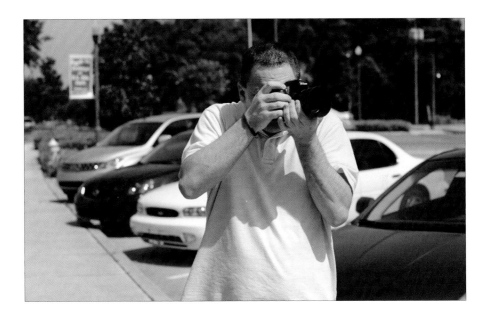

There are many famous photographers who specialize in capturing images of people on the street as they wander around, capturing real life as it happens around them. Unfortunately, these days people are much more aware, and wary, of people taking their photo on the street than ever, but I learned a couple of great tricks from a day I spent wandering the streets of New York City, with living legend Jay Maisel, that can really make a difference. The first was to shoot with a small lens. It can be a zoom lens, but the smaller and less obtrusive the better. Jay pointed out that with shooting on the street, the longer the lens you use, the higher the anxiety (and potential anger) of the people you'll be shooting. With a long lens on your camera, you go from being just another tourist on the street to what they might consider paparazzi, and then things can get ugly. Besides just shooting with a small zoom or fixed focal length lens, Jay told me to "leave the lens hood off," because anything that makes the rig look more pro means more resistance. Another tip was to not look people in the eye when you see the shot you want—don't lock eyes with your subject, just take the shot, and if they look right at you, just smile and move on. Now, of course we were shooting in New York City, where paparazzi are prevalent and people may be more guarded. In most other cities, and in foreign countries, I've found that a nice smile goes a long way and most folks will actually let you take their picture. If you show them the picture on the back of your camera, then they'll usually let you take a whole bunch of shots. The main thing is to respect everybody. If they don't want their photo taken, and they make that known by a facial expression (or a hand gesture, ahem), don't take it.

Get a Model Release

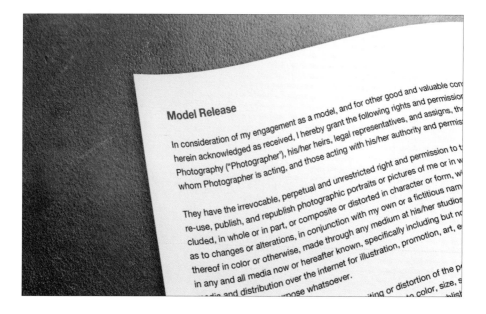

If you're shooting a subject for any commercial use, whether it's a friend or a professional model, make sure you get a signed model release from your subject while they're still in the studio. This release gives you, the photographer, the right to use their likeness in commercial projects like ads, brochures, websites, and promotions, or to resell their images for use in stock photography. You need your subject's written permission on a release to use their photos in this way, because without it you could open yourself up to lawsuits and an embarrassing situation with your client. So, you can avoid all that by getting one signed. Professional models are used to signing model releases (after all, what good would it be if you hired a professional model for a job, and then they wouldn't let you use the pictures for anything?), so that won't generally be a problem whatsoever, and there's no need to feel uncomfortable asking them to sign one. If the subject is a friend or co-worker, just let them know up front that you'll need them to sign a release giving you permission to use their image, and you shouldn't have a problem (I've never had someone I hired or set up an actual shoot with refuse to sign a release). So now that you know you need a release, where do you get one? You can find dozens of free downloadable releases online (just Google "model release"), or you can visit either the Professional Photographers of America (go to ppa.com and search for "model release") or visit the American Society of Media Photographers (ASMP) at http://asmp.org/commerce/legal/releases/ for a great article on releases. The laws regarding releases vary from state to state, and country to country, but having a signed release sure beats not having one.

They Don't Always Need to Be Smiling

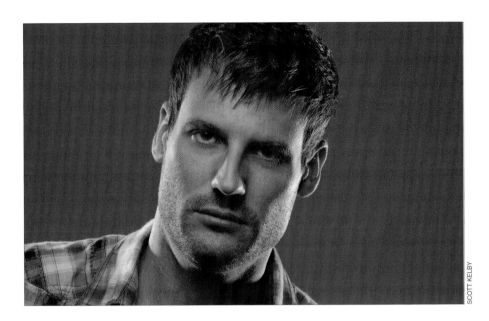

SCOTT KELBY

If we're shooting a portrait, it's our tendency to make sure our subjects are smiling in every shot (after all, you want them to look like they're happy and having a good time, right?). Smiles are great, and we definitely want those shots, but make sure you work some "real" shots in there, too. We're not always smiling in real life, and when we're smiling for a portrait, it's often a posed smile, so you're not capturing a real genuine emotion—you're capturing a fake smile that we've all been doing since we were little kids. If you want to capture portraits that have more depth, more emotion, and more realism, include some shots where your subject isn't smiling (as shown above). If you want your portraits to be more real, this is a great way to open that door.

They Don't All Have to Look at the Camera

Another thing we're programmed to do is always have our subjects facing the camera. While it's true that having your subject's eyes as the main focal point of an image adds interest, some of the most dramatic and captivating portraits ever taken have the subject looking elsewhere. Keep this in mind the next time you're shooting a location portrait, and you might be pleasantly surprised at what you'll come up with.

Overexpose on Purpose

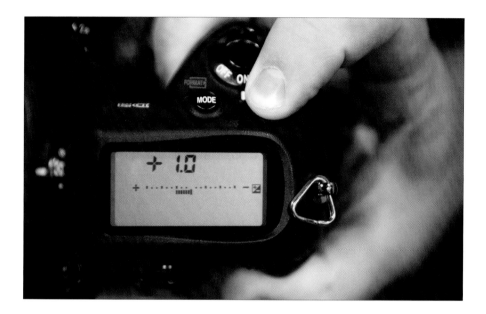

Here's a different look to try: overexpose on purpose. This is great when you want a really bright look for portraits, because it hides detail and gives everything kind of a dreamy, morning-light look to it. Here's how you set this up: go ahead and take a regular shot (let your camera set your exposure), then add some positive exposure compensation, which means you're basically telling the camera, "Okay, I see you picked the right exposure for this photo, but I want to override your choice and make it even brighter." On Nikons, you'd do that by holding the exposure compensation button (the +/– button on top of the camera, right behind the shutter button), then rotating the command dial on the back of the camera until you can see +1 in the control panel on the top of the camera (meaning you just made the exposure one stop brighter than the camera thought it should be). On Canon cameras, first make sure the power switch is set in the top position (above On), then hold the shutter button halfway down, look at the LCD panel on top, and turn the quick control dial to the right to increase the amount of exposure compensation until it reads +1. Now, take a shot and see how the image looks on the LCD monitor on the back of your camera. If it doesn't look bright enough, try increasing the exposure compensation amount and take another test shot (and so on), until it has that dreamy, morning, window light look.

This Doesn't Work in Manual Mode

Exposure compensation works in all the standard modes except manual mode.

Put Multiple Photos Together to Tell a Story

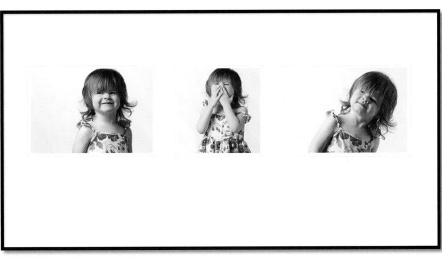

SCOTT KELBY

If you really want to capture a child's personality (and like me, you're not a big fan of the stiff, posed shots), then keep firing while your child is goofing around on the set. Then, take some of the best ones and put three or five together as a series in one frame, like the example shown above. By grouping a set of photos together like this, it instantly goes from a still frame to a story, and I can tell you from experience, clients (parents) just love it!

The Trick to Shooting Newborns and Having Their Faces Not Look So Flat

Newborn babies generally have very flat faces, and that's one reason why it's so hard to get great photos of newborns. The trick is to make their faces look rounder by positioning the baby, or your lighting, so one side of their face is in the shadows. That helps give some depth and dimension, and keeps their face from looking too flat.

Get Out From Behind the Camera for Kids

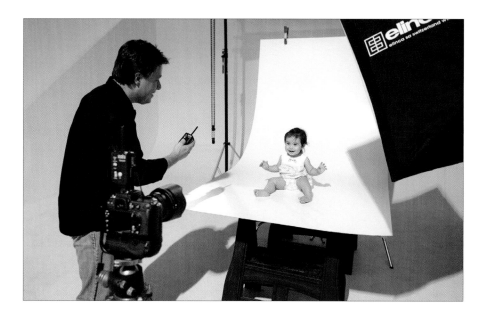

I learned a great trick from Jack Resnicki, a friend who shoots high-end commercial shots of children for print ads and displays in stores (and he's one of the absolute best out there). What Jack does is put the camera in position on a tripod, then rather than being stuck back behind the camera (and putting something between the child and the photographer), he comes right out in front, down on the floor, to get the child engaged. Now you can totally interact with the child, and focus on getting reactions and emotions that are usually so hard to create when your head is buried in the back of a camera. To make this happen, all you need is a wireless shutter release (B&H Photo carries these for all the major brands), and now it's just you and your subject—and you both can focus on the fun that makes such memorable shots.

Only Have One Person Focus the Child's Attention on the Camera

If mom, dad, and grandma are all on the set, they will all try, simultaneously, to get the baby to look at the camera. The problem is that they're usually standing in different areas behind you, so the baby is looking all over the place. Choose one person to be the "attention getter," and have them stand behind and to one side of the camera.

Don't Shoot Down on Kids

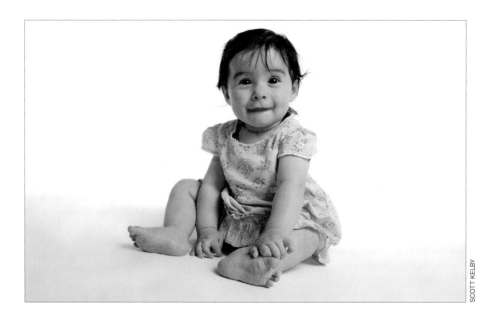

SCOTT KELBY

If you're unhappy with your shots of kids, it may be because you're shooting them like most people do—from a standing position, so basically you're shooting down at them. The problem with this is that, on an average day, that's how we see most children, with us in a standing position looking down at them, and if we photograph them from the same viewpoint, that's how the photos are going to look—average. The trick is to shoot from their level—get down on one knee, or sit (or even lay) on the floor, to capture them from a viewpoint we normally don't see, which honestly changes everything. It's one of the easiest things you can do that will have the greatest impact on your images.

The "Hand Them a Prop" Trick Works Even Better with Kids

If adults get intimidated and shy in front of a camera, imagine how intimidating a studio (with all the lights and stands, etc.) is to a child. To make them relaxed, make it fun by using the same trick you do with adults—give them an interesting or unusual toy or stuffed animal to get their mind off the camera and on the fun.

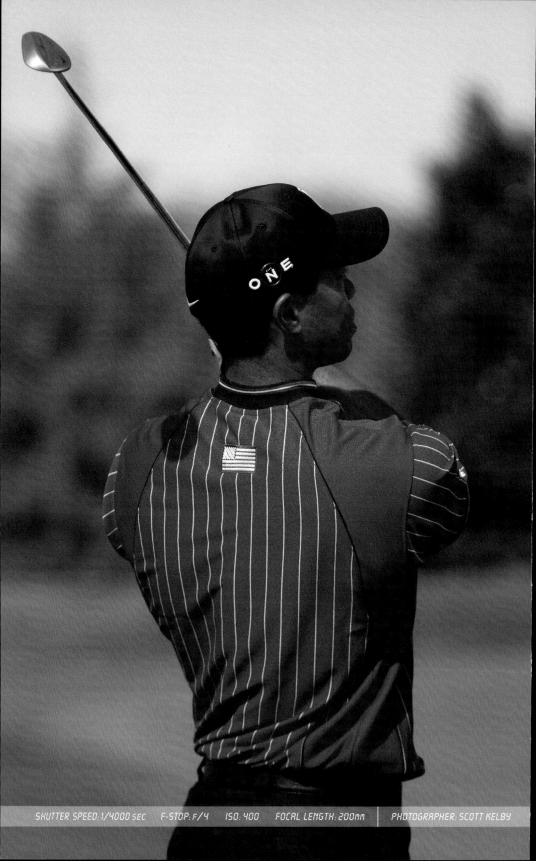

SHUTTER SPEED: 1/4000 SEC   F-STOP: F/4   ISO: 400   FOCAL LENGTH: 200mm   PHOTOGRAPHER: SCOTT KELBY

Chapter Seven

Shooting Sports Like a Pro

How to Get Professional Results From Your Next Sports Shoot

Shooting sports, especially if you have a family member who is one of the participants, is one of the most rewarding, thrilling, exciting, frustrating, maddening, emotionally draining, cuss-word emoting, expensive, laborious, and downright fun things you can do as a photographer. I rank it right up there with accidentally submerging your unprotected camera in saltwater—it's kind of like that. Now, I say this from experience, because these days I spend a good amount of my time shooting professional sports—everything from motorsports to American pro football, from horse racing to baseball—and let me tell you, it's one royal pain in the @$$! So, why do I do it? Because it's a blast! Wait, I just said it's a pain. It is a pain. Just ask any sports shooter. The day after a serious shoot, you're hobbling around like you were actually playing the game instead of just shooting it, but at the same time, there's just nothing like the thrill of shooting sports. Well, it's not all a thrill, there's a lot of what we call "hurry up and wait," because in all sports, there are lots of times where nothing is happening (like timeouts, penalties, breaks between periods or quarters, TV time outs, halftime, someone's hurt on the field, etc.), and you're just standing there talking to other sports photographers who are, by and large, kinda cranky, because it's in those downtime moments when they realize how much they've spent on the equipment required to really shoot sporting events right, and each time they pause to think about it, they die a little inside, because they know they could be driving nice cars, or living in comfortable homes, or they could have sent their kids to a great school, but instead, here they are waiting for the timeout to end, and then they turn to liquor to deaden the pain of a life spent on the road, and before you know it they're writing a volume 3 of their book, when all they really want is a hug, a decent monopod, and a bottle of ibuprofen.

Auto ISO Lets You Always Freeze the Action

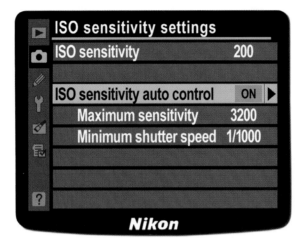

If you're shooting a sport where you need to freeze the action (like football, basketball, baseball, etc.), then you need to make sure you're shooting at a shutter speed that freezes action—around 1/1000 of a second. That's easy to do in broad daylight shooting at a wide open aperture like f/2.8 or f/4 like we would normally do with sports, but if it gets cloudy, or the light changes, or it gets later in the day, you run the risk of your shutter speed falling below 1/1000 and coming home with a bunch of blurry sports shots. That's why you'll fall in love with the Auto ISO feature, which makes sure you never fall below a certain shutter speed, because it will automatically increase the ISO without any input from you. What's especially slick about this is it won't just jump from 200 ISO to 400 ISO, it'll only move exactly as much as it needs, so it might go from 200 ISO to 273 ISO (something you couldn't even choose on your camera if you wanted to, right?). On Nikon cameras, you turn this on by going to the Shooting menu and choosing ISO Sensitivity Settings. Then you enter the Minimum Shutter Speed you want to maintain (I use 1/1000 of a second), and turn the ISO Sensitivity Auto Control on. Now, you get sharp shots every time, no matter how the light changes on the field. On Canon cameras, you need to set the ISO speed to A by looking at the LCD panel and turning the main dial on top of your camera.

Using the Extra Focus Buttons on Long Glass

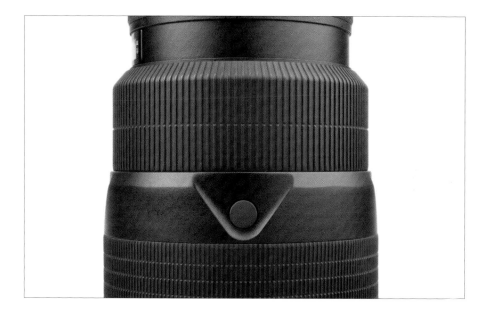

If you're shooting sports with some "long glass" (200mm and on up), on most of these lenses you'll find a second (or multiple) focus button(s) right on the barrel of the lens, down toward the end. These let you use the hand that is steadying the lens to lock in your focus, so when the play happens, you can just press the shutter button quickly. However, there's a little known feature that, when coupled with back focusing, can really make a huge difference in "getting the shot." We'll use baseball as an example. Let's say there's a runner on first, so the play is going to be at second base. Go ahead and focus on second base itself, then turn on the Memory Set button on your long glass (if your lens has a memory lock). Now turn on your camera's back focus (AE Lock) feature, so instead of focusing when you press the shutter button, it focuses when you press the AE Lock button on the back of your camera. Then, swing your camera over to the batter, and press the back autofocus (AE Lock) button to focus on him. When he swings, go ahead and get the shot by pressing the shutter button (you can shoot fast because you don't have to wait for the autofocus to kick in—you already focused with the back autofocus [AE Lock] button). If he gets the hit, swing immediately over to second base, then with your other hand on the barrel, press the second focus button on the barrel of the lens, and it remembers the focus you locked in for second base, so all you have to do is wait for the runner and press the shutter button. Both areas, home plate and second base, will be in perfect focus, and you're right there, ready to capture the action.

Shooting Night Games with Super-High ISO

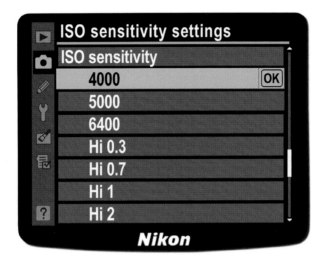

One of the most surprising things that new sports photographers learn is just how dark a playing field is at night. It may look bright from the stands, but for your camera, you might as well be shooting in a museum, because you have to maintain a high enough shutter speed to freeze the action (as I mentioned earlier, a good rule of thumb is 1/1000 of a second). So how big a problem is this? To give you an example, when shooting a Chicago Bears night game at Solider Field in Chicago, I had to shoot at 4000 ISO most of the night to get anywhere near 1/1000 of a second. From the stands, and even when down on the sidelines, it looks incredibly bright, until you look through your viewfinder and see the shutter speed. So, if it's that dim at Solider Field, you can imagine the challenge of shooting a high school football game. That's the reason why cameras capable of shooting at higher ISOs with minimal noise have become so popular (cameras like Canon's Mark III, and Nikon's D700 and D3, have such minimal noise that I'll often shoot at 6400 ISO and the noise is barely noticeable). If you try to shoot at high ISOs like that with lower-end cameras, the noise will be so distracting that you won't get the results you're after. I hate to tell you to rush out and buy an expensive high-ISO camera, but like I said in volume 1 of this book, shooting sports is expensive, so if you're going to do it, you'd better take a second job to pay for your gear.

The Advantage of Shooting From the End Zone

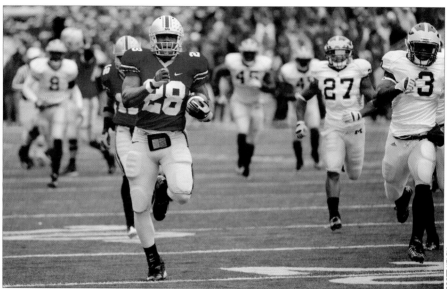

SCOTT KELBY

If you shoot football, you'll probably spend most of your time shooting from the sidelines, and if that's the case, you'll probably spend a lot of your time pulling your hair out as refs, game officials with the first down markers, and TV camera crews (including the guy holding the big parabolic mic dish) all walk into your shots, and block you from getting "the shot." That's why you'll see a lot of pros jockeying for space in the end zone and the corners of the end zone—they usually have a clear, unobstructed line of sight, and they're right in position if someone breaks loose to "take it to the house" (as shown above in this shot I took from the end zone of an Ohio State vs. Michigan game). The only "gotcha" is that if possession changes, you have to decide if you want to go to the opposite end zone, where the plays are now going towards (see, there's always a gotcha!).

The Two Most Popular Sports Shots

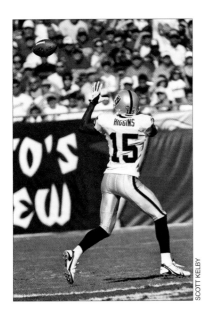

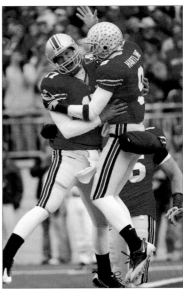

The "Holy Grail" for any serious sports photographer would be to have their work published in *Sports Illustrated* magazine. All the best shooters are there, the images are amazing, and getting to shoot for *SI*, as you'd expect, isn't easy (which is maybe why every sports photographer dreams of doing it). But what kind of images does a magazine like *Sports Illustrated* run the most? I was teaching a class on shooting football and I wanted to answer that question for my class, so I did a little research and I can tell you that, based on that research, they run two types of images: (1) Action images, where the ball (if there is one) is in the frame with the athlete (so if it's a shot of a quarterback or running back, they're holding the ball, or if it's the receiver, he's catching the ball, etc.). (2) Celebrations. Occasionally, it's an editorial shot of an athlete who just suffered a crushing defeat, but usually it's one or more players celebrating after a big win—it's Tiger Woods pumping his fist, a hockey team with their sticks in the air, a soccer player cheering on his knees, two football players bumping chests in midair. Almost invariably, those are the two types of shots that make it into *SI*. Also, they're usually in tight on the players, so you can see their facial expressions and the emotions of the game. So, how does this help you? Well, after all these years, you can imagine that *Sports Illustrated* has figured out exactly which types of sports photos people want to see, right? Right! Now you know which two types of shots you want to be sure to capture the next time you're shooting a game. Remember, if the ball's not in the shot or the players aren't celebrating, it doesn't make it into the magazine. There's a reason.

Once You've Got the Shot, Move On!

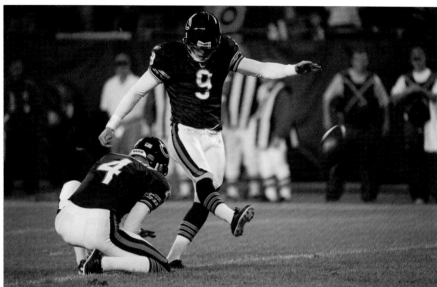

SCOTT KELBY

If you're shooting a game where you're not covering it on assignment, and you don't have a family member actually in the game, here's something to keep in mind: Let's say you're shooting football. Once you've got that great shot of the quarterback, where he's posed in the perfect position, and the ball has just left his hand for a perfect spiral pass, and you framed it just right, and you know you nailed it, or that shot of the kicker going for the extra point, and the ball has just left his foot, but it's still in the frame (as shown here)...move on. Don't keep shooting them doing those moves for the rest of the day expecting something different. I've seen so many times where a friend will shoot a game, and they'll have 200 shots of the quarterback doing essentially the same move. Sometimes they've nailed it in the first round of shots, but they stay on him the rest of the day, shooting literally hundreds of shots. Instead, once you've got "the shot" of that player (the receiver leaping to catch that ball over his head, with the corner's hands trying hopelessly to deflect it), you've got it. You got the shot. Move on to capturing another aspect of the game, another player in another position, or just stick to where the action is. When you get back, you won't just have "the shot." You'll have "the shots!"

Turning Off the Beep

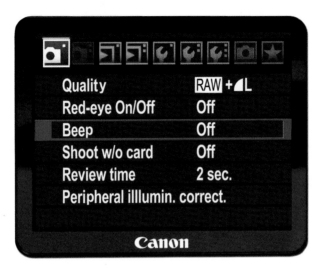

There are certain sports, like tennis or golf, where being quiet and unobtrusive is the name of the game for a photographer (yes, they sometimes will yell at you if you bring any undue attention to yourself), and one simple thing you can do so you don't stick out is to turn off your camera's autofocus beep—that little audible beep that lets you know your autofocus has locked on. Instead, turn that off, then just look in the viewfinder for the visible signal that your focus has locked on (on Nikon cameras, it's the Focus Indicator— the solid round circle on the bottom-left side of the viewfinder. On Canon cameras, it's called the Focus Confirmation Light, and it's found at the bottom right of the viewfinder). That way, the only sound they'll hear is your shutter. To turn off the beep on a Nikon camera, go to the Custom Setting menu, under Shooting/Display, choose Beep, and set it to Off. On Canon cameras, go under the Shooting 1 menu, choose Beep, and set it to Off, as shown above.

Having Your Focus Auto-Track the Action

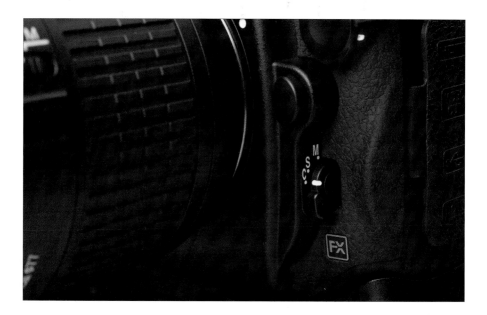

If you're going to be shooting sports, there's a focus setting on your camera that you're going to want to change to help you track the action and stay in focus. Switch from the default focus, which is for non-moving objects, to a focus mode that tries to automatically track a moving object if it moves out of the focus area. On Nikon cameras, you'd switch from Single-Servo mode to Continuous-Servo focus mode, and you do that right on the front of the camera itself—it's that little switch on the front, right under the lens, marked M, S, and C. You want C (for Continuous-Servo). On Canon cameras, it's called AI Servo AF, and you turn it on by pressing the AF•Drive button on the top of the camera, and then turning the main dial until you see AI Servo in the top LCD panel.

Freezing Motion Doesn't Always Look Good

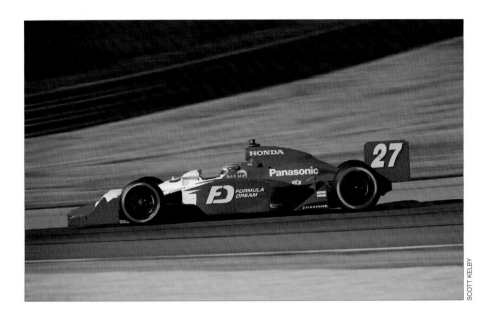

SCOTT KELBY

If you're shooting a sport like car racing, bike racing, or even an air show, freezing the action doesn't always look right. Take car racing, for example. If you completely freeze the action, you won't see the wheels of the car spinning—they'll be frozen like the car was parked on the track, rather than racing around it. Same thing with the wheels on a bike or motorcycle, or the propellers on a stunt plane—they'll all look like they're standing still. The way around this is to lower your shutter speed to around 1/250 to 1/360 of a second, and follow along with the moving object (called panning). That way, the shutter speed will be slow enough to show the wheels (or prop) spinning, and you'll get the sense of motion and speed that would be missing otherwise.

Avoid the Fence at All Costs

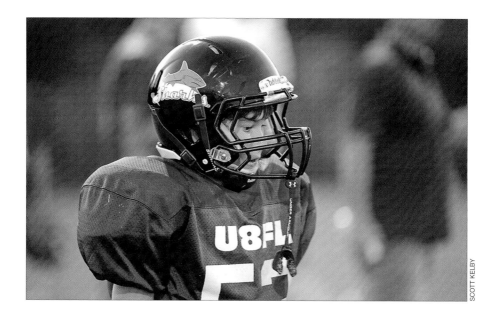

SCOTT KELBY

If you're shooting your kid's game, here's a tip to help you get more professional-looking images: try to set up the shot so instead of seeing a fence (very common), or cars in the parking lot, or the road near the field, you see the crowd (or the other parents, or the other players) in the background. This will look especially good if you're shooting wide open (using the lowest number f-stop your lens will allow, like f/2.8 or f/4), which puts the background out of focus.

Leveraging Daylight to Light Your Players

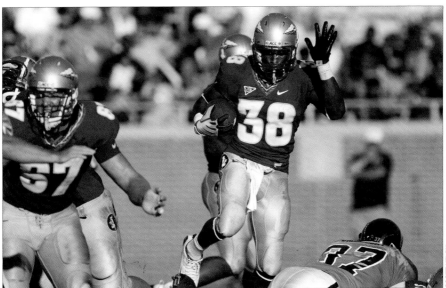

SCOTT KELBY

If you're shooting a game during the day, try to remember to position yourself so the sun is over your shoulder while you're shooting. That way, the players will be lit by the sun, and you'll be able to see their facial expressions. If not, they'll be mostly in the shadows, which is especially bad if they're wearing batting or football helmets. You might have to shoot from the opposite side of the field (which may well be the opposing team's side), but at the end of the day, you'll be able to clearly see all the players, and the emotions that make up the game.

Shoot From a Low Position

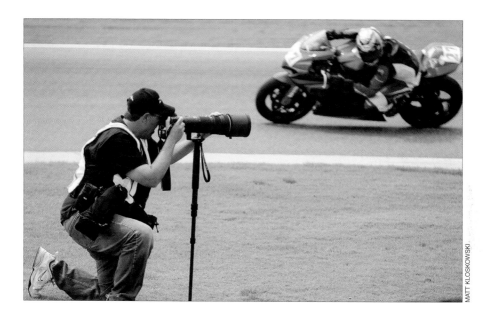

MATT KLOSKOWSKI

The next time you see a sporting event, take a look at the photographers shooting the event, and one thing you'll see again and again is that pros are often shooting down on one knee so they get a lower, and better, perspective for their shots. This goes for everything from motor racing to football—that lower perspective gives you the feeling of being right there, and helps to make the athletes (or their cars) look "bigger than life."

Save Your Knees (You'll Thank Me Later)

Mike Olivella, a pro-sports photographer, turned me on to one of his tricks for saving his knees when shooting at a low perspective: buy some gel-filled knee pads from the local home improvement store. I finally did that a year or so ago, and once I tried them, all I could think was "why did I wait so long?" They're inexpensive, very durable, and every time I wear them, at some point another sports photographer down on his knees looks at me, and through their grimace, says, "I've got to get some of those." Check out page 166 where I've got them on.

Isolate Your Subject for More Impact

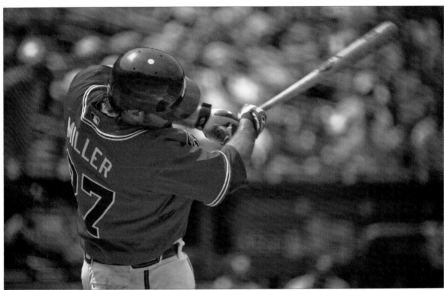

SCOTT KELBY

If you want your sports photos to have more impact, here's another tip to help: try to isolate your subject. There are two ways to do this, the first being simply to frame your shots so that only one or two people appear in the shot (if at all possible). When you get crowds of people in the shot, it's hard for the viewer to tell which person you want them to look at. The last thing you want to do is to make the viewer start searching your photo—trying to find the ball, or the puck. Look for those opportunities to shoot a player in a team sport all by themselves on the field, but during a moment of action. If you're shooting something like soccer or football, you can have more than one player in the frame, but try to make sure your composition makes it instantly clear which player they're supposed to look at, at first glance. The second method is to use a wide-open aperture (f/2.8 or f/4) to put everything in the background out of focus. F/11 is death for sports shots, and even an NFL game can look like a high school game without that shallow depth of field you're used to seeing from the pro shooters. Keep the idea of isolation in mind, and you'll have shots with much more impact your next time out.

Why You Want to Get in Tight

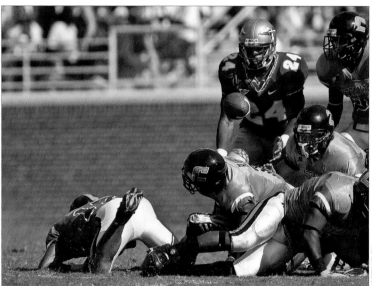

SCOTT KELBY

There's nothing more disappointing for a sports photographer than to have to shoot from the grandstands, and one of the main reasons why is that you'll come away with shots that are very similar to what everybody else in the stands saw that day. You're not bringing anything to them that they couldn't see with their own eyes. That's why it's so important to get in really, really tight when you're shooting sports. That way, you're bringing them something that they can't see with their naked eyes. You're bringing the emotion, the story of the game (not just the score), you're showing the sweat, the anger, the joy, and real things that make sports what it is—not just far off shots of faceless people running around in uniforms. That's why people react so positively to really close-up shots—you're showing them something they don't usually see. It's not just the ordinary view. We don't get that close to the athletes during a game, and seeing this new side of the game is fascinating to the viewer. You're revealing another side of the game by sharing this emotion. That's why we try so hard to get really great access to shoot sporting events. The great shots don't usually come from the stands (unless you've got a really, really long lens, and sadly most major stadiums, at least here in the U.S., are really cracking down on fans bringing pro camera gear to professional sporting events. Many stadiums now have a 4" rule—no lenses longer than 4").

Using a Second Camera Body? Get an R–Strap

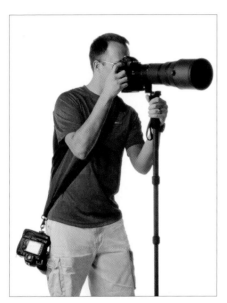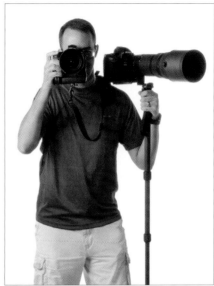

Last year, I was turned on to BlackRapid's R-Strap, which for sports photographers using two camera bodies is a dream come true. (By the way, many pro sports shooters carry two full camera rigs during the event: one with a really long lens, and a second body with a short telephoto or wide-angle for when the action gets really close.) What I love about the R-Strap is that it straps across your chest, and it screws into the bottom of your camera, so your camera kind of hangs there like a gun in a holster (except there's no holster). When you need to take a quick shot with your second body ("quick" being the operative word here), you just reach your hand down to your side, and it falls right into place on your camera—you just pull your camera up to your face, and it slides right along the strap, giving you a fast, comfortable way to get the shot. When you're done, you just put it back down by your side. Being able to reach down and have my second body ready to shoot in a split second is a sports shooter's dream—I wouldn't want to shoot a sports event without it. You can watch a video demo of the R-Strap at www.blackrapid.com.

Tell a Story with Your Shots

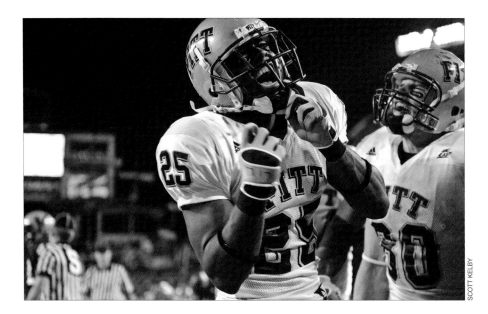

SCOTT KELBY

It's our natural reaction to put down the camera when the play is over, but that is precisely when you want to keep shooting—this is when you get to tell a story with your images. Imagine capturing the look on a quarterback's face when he realizes he's thrown an interception, or when a soccer player is given a red card. How about a coach when they're given what they think is a bad call. That's when the emotion pours out, and if you stop shooting at the end of the play, you'll miss some of the most dramatic, emotional, and even moving, moments in a game—the shots that tell a story.

Full–Frame vs. Standard Digital Chip

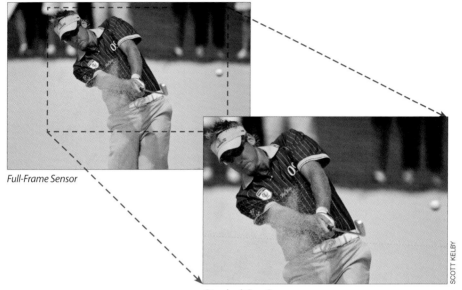

Full-Frame Sensor

Standard-Crop Sensor

SCOTT KELBY

Right now, full-frame sensor cameras are getting all the buzz, but for shooting sports, you might want to consider hanging onto that standard-crop sensor digital camera. Here's why: because of the zoom factor regular-crop sensor digital cameras have, they will get you much closer to the action. For example, a cropped-frame dSLR, like a Nikon D300, will get you 50% closer to the action, or for Canon shooters, an EOS 50D will get you 60% closer than the same lens on a full-frame camera. Here's how that works out: If you put a full-frame 200mm lens on a camera (like a Canon 5D Mark II), you get a real 200mm lens. But put that same 200mm lens on a Canon 50D, and it essentially becomes a 320mm lens. Add a 1.4x tele-converter on that 50D with that same lens, and now you've got nearly a 450mm lens (for the price of a 200mm lens). Landscape photographers make out like bandits with full-frame cameras, because the full-frame sensor lets their wide-angle lenses get much wider. But when it comes to sports, the "old school" 1.5x and 1.6x cropped sensor is very attractive.

High-Speed Crop on a D3 or D700 Is *Not* the Same!

When I talk about this topic, invariably someone asks, "Why don't you use the Nikon D3's built-in high-speed (Auto DX) crop, which switches you to the same cropped-sensor fram-ing as a D300?" It's because using that feature cuts you down from 12-megapixel images to 6-megapixel images, and for sports, you sometimes need to be able to crop in tight after the fact (in Photoshop), and still have enough megapixels to make a high-resolution print, so it's not really an ideal option.

Don't Have "Long Glass?" Rent It for the Week!

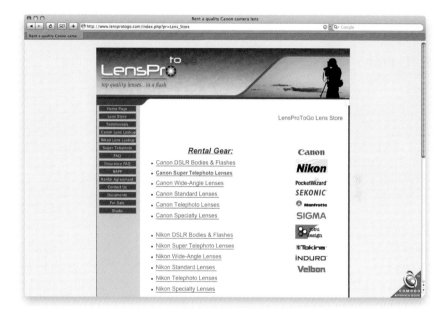

If you have a special game or assignment coming up, and you don't have long enough glass to shoot the game the way you want to, then just rent it. I've done exactly that on a few different occasions from a company called LensProToGo.com. They have all the long glass for both Canon and Nikon shooters (they rent camera bodies, as well), and they ship directly to you overnight. What most people are surprised to find is how reasonably priced they are. For example, to rent a lens like a Nikon 300mm f/2.8 (a great, fast lens for shooting sports) for an entire week is just $230. If that seems like a lot, the alternative is buying that lens. B&H Photo has it in stock (as of this writing) for $4,899.95. So, even though you might not want to rent all the time, when you have a really important game, or a big assignment, they're a great resource (I've rented lenses from them a number of times, and they've always been great—never a problem once).

Still Players Are Boring

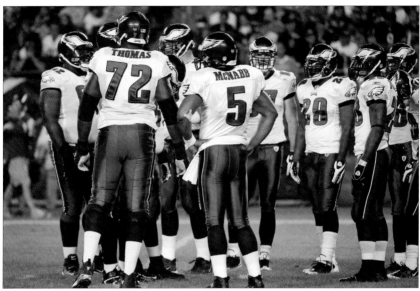

SCOTT KELBY

You'll be there at the game, and you'll see a player getting ready to dash down the field, and you've got a really great angle on them, and so you take the shot. As good as it might have looked in the viewfinder right then, when you open that photo later in Photoshop or Lightroom, you're going to look at that photo and wonder, "What was I thinking?" Don't shoot football players in the huddle or standing around. Don't shoot the runner standing with one foot on first base. Don't shoot the outfielder waiting for a pop fly—wait until the ball is there. Shoot the action, because when you start looking at your photos later, you're going to hate the shots that don't have it.

Another Reason to Keep Shooting After the Play

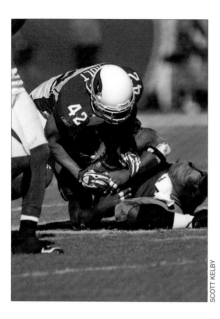

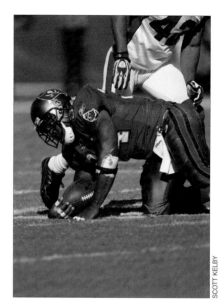

If you're shooting a team sport like football, it's easy to have the player you just shot carrying the ball, lost in a big pile of jerseys. Who was that player? Was it #22 or #37? If you keep shooting for a few moments after the play is whistled dead, you'll be able to see who finally comes up with the ball, and you'll have a reference photo with their number on it, so you can figure out later who the ball carrier on that play actually was. In the example shown here, when the player started getting up (shown on the right), I could see his number on the top of his shoulder pad (#34).

Add a Battery Grip for More Frames Per Second

You can get more frames per second with certain Nikon cameras (like the D300 or D700) by adding a battery grip. Adding one (and using the proper battery configuration) increases your fps rate, sometimes pretty significantly. For example, adding a battery grip to a Nikon D700 increases the fps from five frames per second to eight frames per second. That's a 60% increase in frame rate (not to mention that with a battery grip, you now have a shutter button on top for shooting vertical, which believe me, makes all the difference in the world).

You Don't Have to Drag Around a Camera Bag

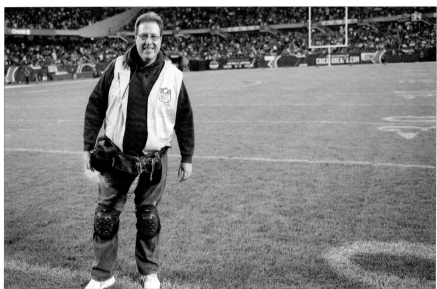

BILL SMITH

With all the gear you'll be carrying around to shoot a sporting event, the last thing you want to have to do is lug around your camera bag. Worse yet, if you do bring it with you, you have to keep a close eye on it all day, because while you've got your eye in the view-finder, someone else could have their eye on your expensive gear. You get the shot, they get your other camera and lenses. That's one reason why a couple of years ago I switched to Think Tank Photo's Modular belt system, where my spare lenses, accessories, memory cards, water bottle, and even my cell phone are all just inches away, because they're right there wrapped around me, attached to a belt. Their system does an amazing job of distributing the weight, and like most sports shooters who use these (and there are a lot) will tell you, you completely forget you have it on. When you buy one of these, you can choose which types of lens pouches you want (they have sizes to fit all your regular lenses), which types of accessory pouches you want, and basically you just customize this belt system to your gear and your needs. I don't know a single sports shooter who has bought one of these that doesn't swear by it. Go to www.thinktankphoto.com to see what it's all about.

Start Shooting Right Before the Game

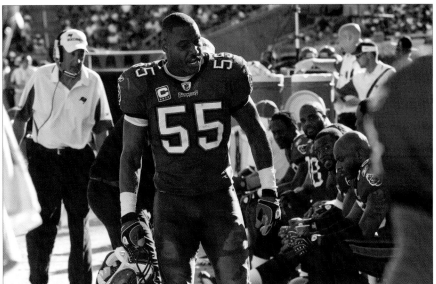

SCOTT KELBY

Right before a big game, the energy level is really high, and different athletes deal with this rush/stress/excitement in different ways. Some are all pumped up, and they're trying to fire up the other players, and some are very serious and quiet at moments like this, as they mentally prepare for the battle. This time, just a few minutes before the game, is a great time to catch some very emotional images right along the sidelines, or in the tunnel, or outside the locker room. Keep an eye out for capturing the different personalities and how they're reacting to what's about to happen, and you might come away with some killer shots before the opening whistle even blows.

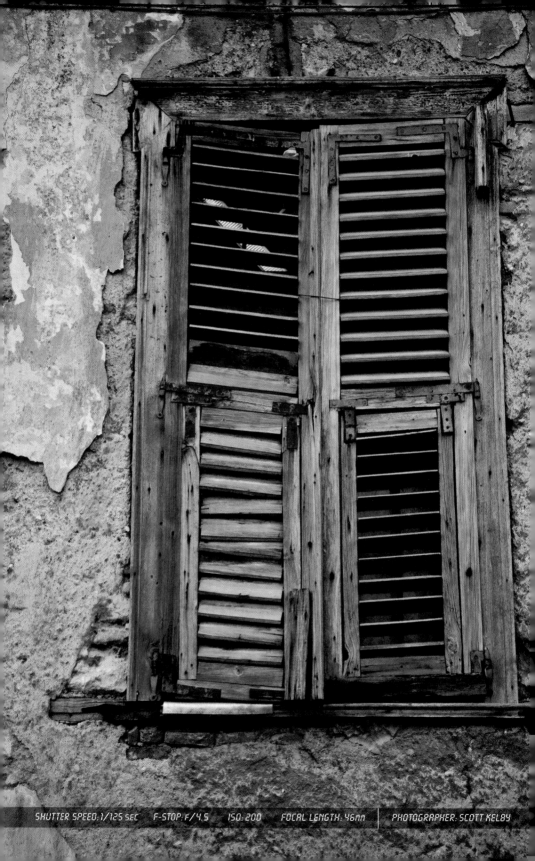

Chapter Eight

Pro Tips for Getting Better Photos

Tricks of the Trade for Making All Your Shots Look Better

Each of the other chapters in this book teaches you techniques that are pretty specific to a particular type of photography (like portraits, or shooting in the studio, etc.), but I wanted to once again include a collection of techniques that is just simply about getting better shots. At the end of the day, that's all we really want, right? We just want to take better photos. It's why we all work so hard to learn how to use our cameras—not so we can play around in the menus all day, it's because we know that once we really know the camera inside and out, then we can focus on getting the shots (and not the technology behind it all). Now, I know what you're probably thinking, "Scott, this all makes perfect sense, except for one thing: I'm reading this in one of the chapter introductions, and traditionally this is a part of the book that's not widely known for contributing to the chapter that lies ahead. What gives?" Well, here's the thing: my statement above would all make perfect sense if the chapter that follows was actually about making your photos look better, but sadly, it's not. What follows is actually a 22-page excerpt from my doctoral dissertation on neo-classical psychology patterns, which includes a non-apologetic look at man's inability to reconcile events from his pre-post-natal experiences and how those events have affected his non-verbal communication skills in the post-modern workplace. The reason I'm sharing this excerpt with you here is because I feel it deserves a wider audience than just my professor, who incidentally did not agree with several of the conclusions put forth in my well-documented, thoroughly researched, and flawlessly executed paper, which is why he will be referred to throughout the upcoming chapter as simply "Professor Big Poopie Head." Now, if you're thinking, "Dr. Kelby, I didn't know you had earned a doctorate," just remember this one underlying rule: I'm lying.

Using Live View to Set Your White Balance

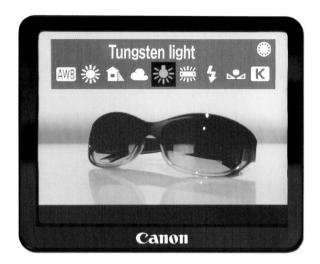

There is a very cool new feature in some of the latest Nikon and Canon dSLRs that lets you use the LCD monitor on the back of the camera as a viewfinder, so you can compose and shoot your image using just it (just like a point-and-shoot camera). Now, it may not sound that appealing, but check this out: on some of these newer cameras, when you're view-ing the scene on your LCD, you can actually toggle through the different white balance settings and see right then and there how each white balance setting is going to look for that particular scene. This makes dialing in a great looking white balance absolutely simple—just scroll through the list, and when you see one that looks good, stop. Try it once, and you'll use it again and again (especially easy when you're on a tripod).

Spot Metering

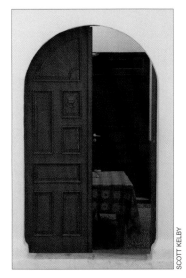 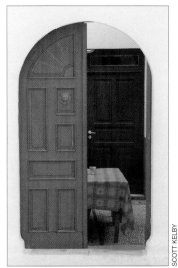

Before   *After*

Most folks keep their camera's metering set at the default, which is evaluative metering (on Canons) or matrix metering (on Nikons) and that just means it kind of looks at the entire frame and it tries to create an exposure that works for the entire image. These modes, on today's cameras, do a pretty amazing job most of the time. However, there's another type of metering—spot metering—you'll want to know about for those sticky exposures, like in the image above left, where I'm trying to capture both the light inside the little entryway and outside the building at the same time. In the default evaluative (or matrix) metering mode, it's going to make that entryway very dark. So, just switch to spot metering mode. This essentially tells the camera, "the part of the photo I want to look good is just this little tiny area right in the center of the frame." Then, you aim the center of the frame directly at that area, hold the shutter button down halfway to lock in that exposure reading, then reframe your photo to look how you want it (without releasing that shutter button), and take the photo. In the example above right, I just switched from matrix metering to spot, then aimed at the table inside that doorway. That's all it took (just remember to switch back to matrix, or evaluative, metering when you're done, because you generally only want to use spot metering in tricky exposure situations).

Shooting Concerts and Events

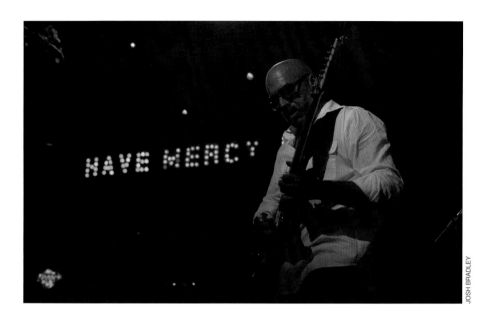

JOSH BRADLEY

One of the biggest mistakes people make when shooting concerts or events is to try to use their flash. A friend of mine shot a concert once and hated the results he got (he used flash). He emailed me some of the images, and I saw exactly why. I wrote him back, "So let me get this straight—there were around 275 of these huge 1,000-watt stage lights aiming right at the performers, but you thought there just needed to be one more?" We laughed about it, but there's a lot of truth to it. You want to see the color and vibrance of the stage lights, and you want the scene you photograph to look like what it looked like when you were there at the concert. Using flash wipes all that out (besides making the performers angry), and reveals all sorts of distracting things like cables, cords, plugs, duct tape, etc., that would never have been seen under normal stage lighting (in fact, if you shoot big name acts, they forbid the use of flash, and you generally only get to shoot for the first three songs of the concert, if that!). Since you absolutely shouldn't use flash, the key is to shoot at a high enough ISO that you can get your shutter speed around 1/125 of a second (to give you sharp shots in lower light—and yes, the stage is often very dramatically lit, and the lights are constantly changing, which is why shooting performances is so tricky). Since you may get some noise at these higher ISOs, be prepared to use a noise reduction plug-in (I've been using Nik Software's Dfine 2.0), and take along the fastest (lowest possible f-stop) lenses you've got (f/2.8, f/2, f/1.8, etc.). If you're close to the stage, take both a wide-angle lens and something like a 70–200mm f/2.8, or even an f/4 if you've got a good, low-noise camera.

Shooting Home Interiors

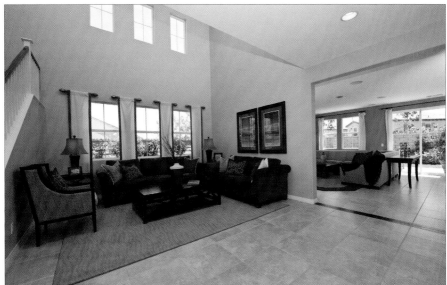

SCOTT KELBY

If you want better looking home interior shots, here are a few things to do that will make a big difference: First, turn on all the lights in the room (turn on every single light you can). This isn't to add light to the scene—this is to give the room some life (realtors have home-owners do the same thing when they're showing the house to prospective home buyers). Now, you have two jobs: (1) To make the room look big. Nobody wants to see a tiny little room, and one trick for doing that is to shoot down low, from a kneeling position, with a wide-angle lens. Then position your camera so you're aiming into one of the room's cor-ners. One of the biggest ideas to get your head around is what to do with bright window light coming into the room, because your camera isn't going to properly expose for what's inside the room and what's outside the window at the same time. So, here's what you need to consider: First, it's now fairly acceptable to let what's outside the window completely blow out to white (you even see this now in fine home magazines, so don't let it freak you out). If you feel that what's outside is as important as what's inside, then you need to take two shots with two separate exposures—one exposed for the room interior, then a sec-ond where you expose for what's visible through the window, and just ignore how dark the interior looks in this second shot. Then you put these two separate exposures together in Photoshop (yup, I did a video for you on that, too, at www.kelbytraining.com/books/digphotogv3). Now, (2) the final challenge (hey, I didn't say this was easy) is to evenly light the room. Most pros use one or more small off-camera flashes, hidden behind furniture (so you don't see them) and aimed straight up at the ceiling, to evenly light the room.

Shooting Time-Lapse Photography (Canon)

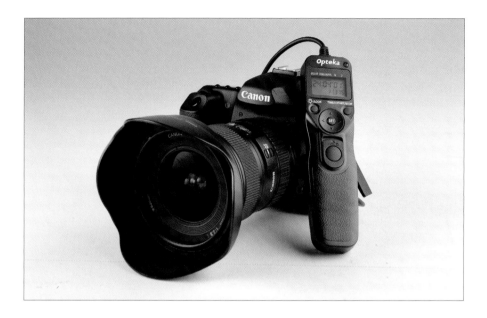

If you've ever watched a concert video, they always seem to have a video segment at the beginning where you see an empty venue, and then you watch while a giant stage, with tons of lights and speakers, is constructed right before your eyes—something that took an entire day or two to construct in real time, but here the whole experience lasts maybe 30 seconds total. This technique is called time-lapse photography (you've seen this used on TV to show a setting sun, outdoor events, a flower opening, etc.) and to do this, you set your camera on a tripod, and have the camera take a shot at a regular interval (like every 30 seconds, or every minute, etc.) over a certain period of time (like an hour, a day, two weeks, etc.), and then you combine all these images into a movie on your computer (I did a how-to video for you at www.kelbytraining.com/books/digphotogv3). Now, if you're doing this over a short period of time, you can just pull out a stopwatch, and every so many seconds or minutes, take a shot. However, for longer periods, if you're shooting a Canon camera, you'll need a separate timer accessory like Canon's TC80N3 Timer Remote Control, which costs around $140, which is why you probably want the Opteka Timer Remote Control instead (for around half the price). Either one connects to your camera's 10-pin input and lets you choose how many shots, how often, and over what length of time to capture your images. Now just start it, and walk away (well, walk away, providing of course, that your camera gear is safe and won't get stolen).

Shooting Time–Lapse Photography (Nikon)

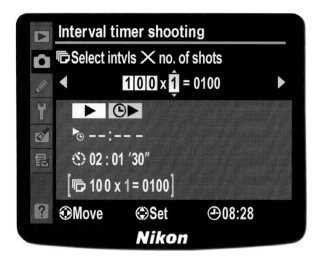

If you've ever watched a concert video, they always seem to have a video segment at the beginning where you see an empty venue, and then you watch while a giant stage, with tons of lights and speakers, is constructed right before your eyes—something that took an entire day or two to construct in real time, but here the whole experience lasts maybe 30 seconds total. This technique is called time-lapse photography (you've seen this used on TV to show a setting sun, outdoor events, a flower opening, etc.) and to do this, you set your camera on a tripod, and have the camera take a shot at a regular interval (like every 30 seconds, or every minute, etc.) over a certain period of time (like an hour, a day, two weeks, etc.), and then you combine all these images into a movie on your computer (I did a how-to video for you at www.kelbytraining.com/books/digphotogv3). A number of Nikon dSLRs have this feature built right in (like the D3, D300, and D700), so all you have to do is put your camera on a tripod, then go under the Shooting menu and choose Interval Timer Shooting. Press the right arrow, and choose when you want your interval timer (time-lapse) shooting to begin, how often you want a photo taken, the number of intervals, and the number of shots per interval. Now choose On and then OK, and you can walk away and the camera will record the images for you automatically (of course, don't just walk away if you feel like someone might walk up and take your camera).

Creating Multiple Exposures

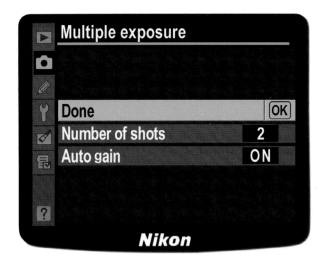

If you want to combine two separate images into one single frame, there are two ways to do it: in-camera (if you own a Nikon dSLR) or in Photoshop, after the fact (for Canon or other dSLR users that don't have built-in multiple exposures). For the Nikon folks: You turn this feature on by going under the Shooting menu and choosing Multiple Exposure, then Number of Shots, and picking how many images you want to combine into one single image (in the example above, I just chose two), then choose OK. If you want a consistent background for both shots, put the camera on a tripod. Take the first shot, then have your subject move to a new position on the other side of the frame (don't let them move so far away that they're out of the frame), and take your second shot. That's it—both images will appear in the same frame (the advantage of doing it in-camera is that you have the two images combined as a single RAW file vs. doing this in Photoshop, where the end result will have to be a JPEG, TIFF, or PSD. If you're not shooting Nikon, I did a little video to show you how to combine two photos using Photoshop. You'd still have to start by taking two separate photos of your subject, and then we'll combine those in Photoshop. You can find this video at www.kelbytraining.com/books/digphotogv3.

Do You Really Need to Read Your Histogram?

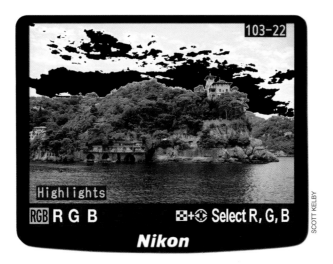

This may be the most shocking thing you read in this book: not only do I not use the histogram on the back of the camera, but most of the pros I know don't either. With digital photography, our main concern is keeping detail in the highlight areas of our photo (so the brightest parts of our photo don't get so bright that there's nothing there but solid white), so instead of trying to evaluate the histogram, we just turn on our camera's highlight warning. It warns us if any part of our image is clipping (losing highlight detail), so then we can use exposure compensation to override the exposure our camera chose, and darken the exposure a bit until the detail comes back. That warning is telling us that the right side of the histogram is hitting the right wall of the graph (known as the "right wall of death" by…well…me). Anyway, here's why the highlight warning is better: the histogram only tells me if some part of the photo is hitting that right wall, it doesn't tell me if what's hitting the wall is something I care about, whereas the highlight warning shows me, right on the LCD monitor, exactly what part of my image is clipping, so I can quickly see if it's an area of important detail (like a white shirt) or something that doesn't have detail (like the sun. In the example shown above, you can see by all the black in the sky that these areas are clipping). So, if you're spending a lot of time worrying about your histogram, or worse yet, worrying that you don't know what the histogram even is, now you can get a good night's sleep. *Note*: Some people get really fanatical about technical stuff like histograms, so I just want to clarify this: I'm not telling you not to use your histogram, I'm just telling you that I don't use it. (Wink, wink.)

Using an Online Photo Lab

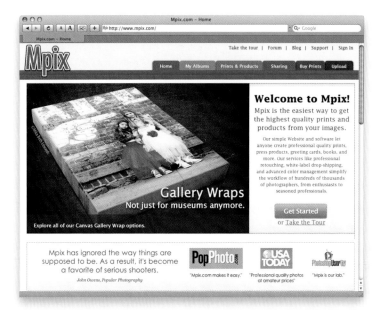

Back when I was shooting film, I used to send my most important shoots to a professional film lab for processing, but once digital photography (and great inexpensive printers) came along, I started doing all my own printing. Today, I do both. I still do some of my own printing, but I also often use an online lab for five reasons: (1) It's just so darn fast and easy. I upload the photos using my Web browser, and if I upload the images to the lab I use before lunch, they print and ship them the same day. (2) They'll color correct all my photos for free (I'm pretty handy in Photoshop, but sometimes it's just faster to let somebody else do it). (3) They can print in sizes that perfectly match the size digital cameras produce (so there's no cropping of my images to fit outdated sizes like 8x10" or 11x14". (4) You can have your prints mounted, matted, and framed (with glass), and (5) you can choose different types of paper (including metallic prints, matte finishes, etc.). This is one of those things that once you try it, you'll wonder why you waited so long. Plus, today's pricing for online labs is very competitive.

Mpix.com Is the Only Online Lab I Use

I've used Mpix.com since 2007, but had no idea how many Mpix freaks were out there until I mentioned them on my blog. People came out of the woodwork to tell me about their love affair with Mpix, and now I know why. They're not just for pros—anybody can use Mpix—but their quality makes you look like a pro. Try them once, and you'll see what I mean.

Shooting in Tricky Low-Light Situations

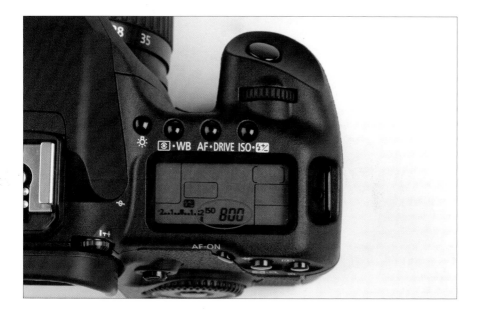

Although there are some tried and true techniques for shooting in tricky low-light situations (like shooting in a cave, or at your daughter's dance recital, or around a campfire), unfortunately there is no secret setting or magic button that suddenly makes it all work. However, here's what you can do: The #1 thing you can do is to find a way to steady your camera. Because you're in really low light, your shutter speed is going to drop way below 1/60 of a second (as low as most of us can hand-hold and still get a reasonably sharp photo), so ideally, you're going to need to put your camera on a tripod. If you can't use a tripod, how about a monopod? If you don't have either, rest your camera on something (I've been known to balance my camera on the seat back of an empty theater chair, or on a railing at a tourist attraction, or on the safety wall at the top of the Empire State Building in New York. I've even put the camera on a friend's or family member's shoulder to steady it). I do everything I can to steady it to avoid having to raise the ISO (which is our last resort, unless you have one of the new high-end cameras with great low-noise results at high ISOs). If there's just no way to steady your camera, then you have to resort to raising your ISO—keep raising it until you get your shutter speed to 1/60 of a second or higher, and then hold your camera as still as possible. If you raise your ISO up quite a bit, you're going to see noise in your photos, so you're going to need to run some noise reduction software (I've been using Nik Software's Dfine 2.0, a Photoshop and Lightroom plug-in, which does an amazing job of reducing the noise without blurring your photo too much).

Shooting Night Scenes Like Cityscapes

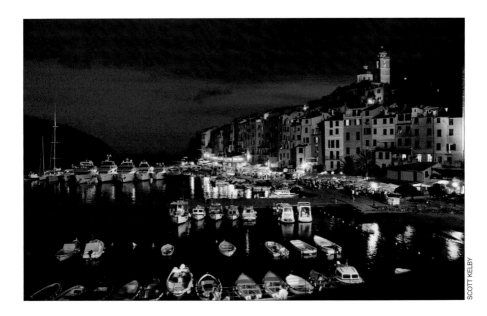

SCOTT KELBY

Shooting nighttime scenes is kinda tricky, because no two scenes are lit the same. However, here are some tips to help: The most important thing is getting the right exposure. Since everything is so dark, your first thought might be to aim at the lights, but if you do, your camera will think the whole scene is bright, and it will greatly underexpose your photo. Instead, try focusing just to the left or right of the lights. Take a shot and check your LCD monitor. If it still looks too dark, use exposure compensation to brighten the image by one stop, then take another test shot. It won't take long before you nail the exposure. Also, your exposure time will go anywhere from a few seconds to a few minutes (depending on how much light the scene you're shooting has), so you absolutely must be on a tripod to get a sharp shot. Since your shutter will be open for a long time, you'll also want to use a cable release or wireless shutter release, so you don't add any movement at all by pressing the shutter button with your finger. For getting a white balance that looks good, I use the Live View white balance trick on page 170. One last thing: the best time to shoot nighttime cityscapes is about a half-hour past sunset, so you get the perfect mix of natural light and city lights.

Remove Your UV Filter for Nighttime Shots

When it comes to shooting at night, this is the one time when the limited ultraviolet (UV) rays work against us (potentially giving us washed out images), and that's why many pros suggest removing your UV filter when shooting at night.

How My Camera Is Usually Set Up

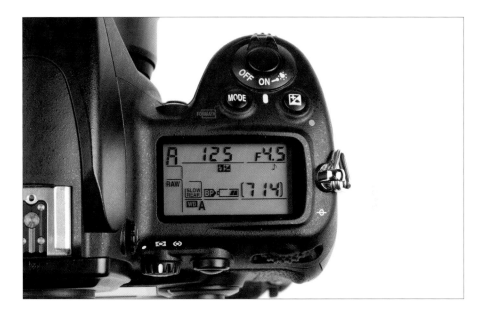

I set up my camera pretty much the same way each time I shoot. First, I nearly always shoot in aperture priority mode, because I can choose whether I want the background behind my subject to be out of focus or sharp and in focus. This works whether I'm shooting sports, or a bee on a flower, or a sweeping landscape shot—I have total creative control over how the background looks. The only other shooting mode I use is manual, and then only when I'm in the studio using studio strobes. I try to shoot at ISO 200 as much as possible (it's always my starting place), and I only raise it if my shutter speed falls below 1/60 of a second (that's about as slow as I can go hand-holding my camera and still get a sharp shot. Some folks can go to 1/30, but not me). If I'm shooting out in daylight (like on a vacation trip or at an outdoor sporting event), I leave my white balance set on Auto. If I wander into the shade, I change it to Shade, and if I walk inside, I match the white balance to the lighting I'm shoot-ing in (this keeps me from having to color correct my photos later). I leave my camera's flash setting at Rear-Curtain Sync (2nd Curtain for Canon users) all the time (that way, I get some movement around my subject, but then the flash fires to freeze them and make them sharp). I leave the highlight warning turned on all the time, and refer to it often (so I don't blow out my highlights). I never look at the histogram (sorry).

What I Pack for a Landscape Shoot

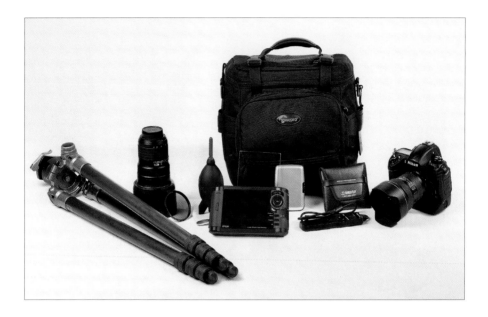

If I'm heading out for a landscape shoot, here's what I pack:

(1) One full-frame camera body (I take a full-frame body when shooting landscapes to get wider images)
(2) A 14–24mm f/2.8 ultra-wide-angle lens
(3) A good sturdy tripod with a ballhead
(4) One medium zoom lens, in case I want to shoot a panorama (I avoid wide-angle lenses when shooting panos)
(5) A cable release (either a wired release or, ideally, a wireless release)
(6) A polarizer (to cut reflections and darken the sky)
(7) A split neutral density gradient filter (to let me expose for the foreground and not have the sky get washed out)
(8) An Epson P-3000, -6000, or -7000 for backing up my images when out in the field
(9) A neutral density filter (to darken a waterfall or stream scene, so I can use a long enough shutter speed to make the water look silky)
(10) A backup battery, my battery charger, a cleaning cloth (in case I get water droplets on my lens), and a Rocket Air Blower (to blow any dust or specks off my lens)
(11) Multiple memory cards in a hard-sided memory card case
(12) It all goes in a LowePro Pro Mag 2 AW

What I Pack for a Sports Shoot

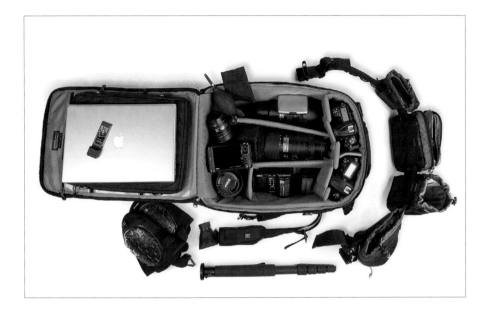

If I'm heading out for a sports shoot, here's what I pack:

(1) Two camera bodies

(2) A very long lens, like a fast 200–400mm f/4 zoom lens, or a 300mm fixed focal length lens

(3) A zoom lens, like a 70–200mm f/2.8, and one wide-angle zoom, like a 24–70mm

(4) A fisheye lens (in case I want to get a shot of the stadium, arena, etc.)

(5) A monopod to support my longest lens

(6) A BlackRapid R-Strap for my second camera body, so I can bring my second camera up to fire quickly if I need it

(7) An Epson P-3000, -6000, or -7000 for backing up my images when out in the field

(8) A laptop and a fast FireWire (or IEEE 1394) memory card reader

(9) A wireless PC card for uploading photos while the event is still underway

(10) Backup batteries for both bodies, battery chargers, a cleaning cloth, and a Rocket Air Blower to blow any dust or specks off my lens

(11) Gel kneepads (to save my knees when kneeling to get a low perspective for sports photography)

(12) A Think Tank modular belt system that holds my fisheye lens, backup memory cards, a water bottle, an energy bar, and my wide-angle lens

(13) A Hoodman HoodLoupe (which covers my LCD, so I can see it clearly in bright daylight)

(14) It all fits into a Think Tank Airport Security 2 rolling camera bag

What I Pack for a Location Portrait Shoot

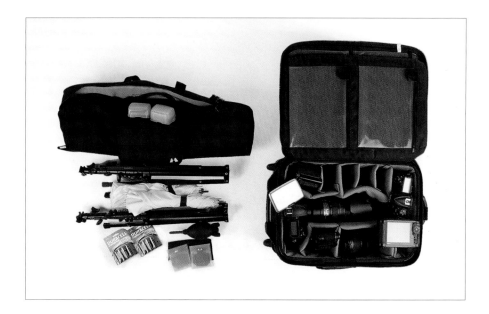

If I'm heading out for a location portrait shoot, here's what I pack:

(1) A 70–200mm zoom lens

(2) A 24–70mm zoom lens

(3) Two off-camera wireless flashes with diffusion domes

(4) Two lightweight 7' light stands, two shoot-through umbrellas, and two tilt bracket adapters

(5) Two 8-packs of AA batteries (for the flash units)

(6) Two sets of gels for the flashes: one orange, one green

(7) A separate battery pack to get faster refreshes from the flash units

(8) An Epson P-3000, -6000, or -7000 for backing up my images when out in the field

(9) Multiple memory cards in a hard-sided memory card case

(10) One camera body, and a backup body if it's a paying gig

(11) A backup battery, my battery charger, a cleaning cloth, and a Rocket Air Blower to blow any dust or specks off my lens

What I Pack for a Travel Shoot

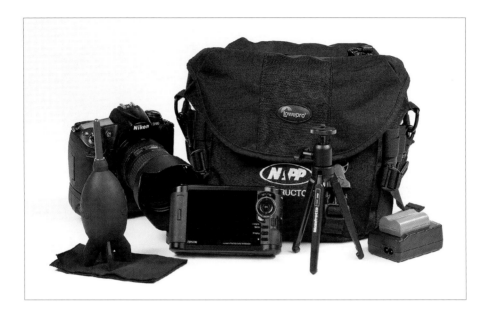

If I'm heading out for a travel shoot while I'm on vacation, here's what I pack:

(1) One camera body (a regular cropped-frame body)

(2) An 18–200mm zoom lens (I want one lens that does it all)

(3) An Epson P-3000, -6000, or -7000 for backing up my images when out in the field

(4) A backup battery, my battery charger, a cleaning cloth, and a Rocket Air Blower to blow any dust or specks off my lens

(5) A small tabletop tripod, so I can shoot food or sneak in a shot where full-sized tripods aren't usually allowed

What I Pack for a Wedding Shoot

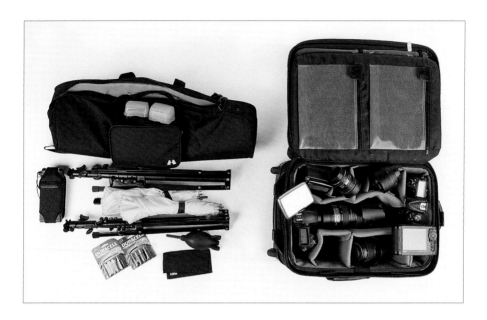

If I'm heading out for a wedding shoot, here's what I pack:

(1) Two camera bodies (the extra one is a backup)

(2) A 14–24mm super-wide-angle lens, a 50mm f/1.4 lens (for shooting hand-held in low light), a 70–200mm f/2.8 VR zoom lens, a 10.5mm fisheye lens (great for capturing fun at the reception), and a 24–70mm f/2.8 lens

(3) An Epson P-3000, -6000, or -7000 for backing up on-site and four 8-GB memory cards

(4) A lens cleaning kit

(5) This all fits in a LowePro Pro Roller 1 Bag

Lighting Gear:

(1) Two off-camera flashes (like Nikon SB-900s)

(2) Diffusion domes for the flash units

(3) A Nikon SU-800 commander unit (to fire the flashes wirelessly)

(4) Two Bogen light stands with umbrella swivel brackets (the second one is a backup)

(5) Two Westcott 43" shoot-through white translucent umbrellas (the second is a backup)

(6) A Westcott white/silver reflector

(7) A tri-grip diffuser

(8) Four packs of AA batteries, AA battery charger, and a Nikon SD-9 battery pack (for longer battery life and faster refresh times)

(9) A ladder cart (to shoot up higher, and to lug the lighting gear around)

(10) I pack my flashes, stands, umbrellas, and brackets all in one Hakuba PSTC 100 Tripod Case

White Balance vs. Color Correction

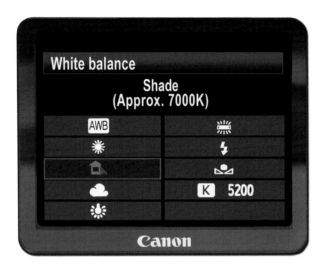

If you're wondering why you hear so much these days about getting a proper white balance when you're shooting, here's why: if you get the white balance right in the camera, you won't have to do any color correction later in Photoshop (or Lightroom, or Aperture, or whatever). That's because, if the white balance is properly set, the color of the photo will look spot on. If the white balance is off, you're going to have to do some color correction later or your photo will look too blue, too yellow, too green, etc., so if you want to avoid the whole color correction process, just set your camera's white balance setting to the type of light you're shooting in (for example, if you're shooting in the shade, set your camera's white balance to Shade. Yes, it is that easy).

If You Want to Nail Your White Balance Every Time, Get an ExpoDisc

Switching your white balance in-camera to match the type of lighting you're shooting in will definitely get you closer than not doing it, but if you really want to nail the white balance every time, you need something like an ExpoDisc (from ExpoImaging). This is a translucent disc you hold over the end of your lens, aim at the light source, then take a photo, and it creates a custom white balance for you that is designed for the exact light you're shooting in. They do work wonders, and lots of pros swear by them.

How Many Great Shots to Expect From a Shoot

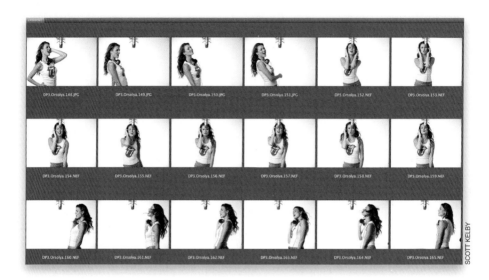

SCOTT KELBY

So, if you're a pretty serious photographer and you come back from a few hours of shooting (let's say you were on a photowalk, or wandering around a city while on vacation), and you took, say…240 shots, how many of those should you expect to be really killer shots— shots you would enlarge, frame, and hang on the wall? A lot of folks are surprised (actually shocked) to learn that even most pros would be happy to come away with one really great shot from that 240. Personally, if I can get two or three from that shoot that I really like, I am thrilled. Think of it this way: if you were hired to shoot the cover shot for *Vogue* magazine, and you hired a top model and assistants and a big New York or Paris studio, and you shot all day long and took thousands of shots, how many of those would wind up on the cover? One. Realistically, how many would the folks at *Vogue* really have to choose from, from your shoot? How many shots would you have captured that were "cover of *Vogue*" quality? Even a top pro might have 10 or 12 really great cover-quality shots for them to choose from. This is true for landscape photographers, travel photographers, commercial photographers—all of us. Talk to some of the top pros and you'll find that most of their shots go in the trash, but when they shoot 240 photos, there are usually a few really great ones in there, too—some killer shots—but how many of those will they actually frame and put on the wall? Maybe one. When you see a pro's work on display (in a gallery or a slide show presentation), you're seeing only their very best work. You're seeing nothing but that one killer shot from that day. They've just done a lot of those 240-image shoots.

If Your Camera Shoots Video....

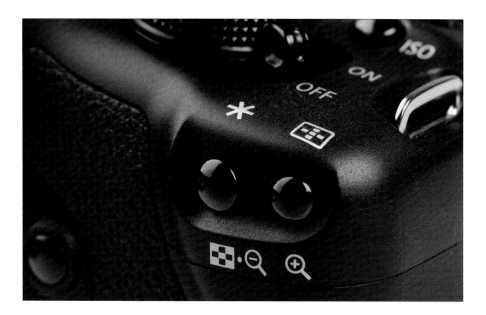

If your dSLR has the ability to shoot high-definition video, like a Canon 5D Mark II or a Nikon D90 or D5000 (by the way, more and more dSLR cameras are getting video these days), then there's a special setting that will help you get much better results from shooting video. You want to lock the Auto Exposure setting, or as you pan across a room or a scene, the exposure will keep trying to change as you pan, so during your pan the video starts glowing brighter then darker then brighter again (ugh!). On Nikon cameras, go under the Custom menu, to Controls, and choose Assign AE-L/AF-L Button (those acronyms stand for Auto Exposure Lock and Auto Focus Lock). Then, scroll down to AE Lock (Hold) and choose that. Now, when you're shooting video, once you start shooting, you'll press the AE-L/AF-L button on the back of the camera, and it will hold your exposure in place while you're panning the camera. Press it a second time to turn auto exposure lock off. On a Canon dSLR with video (other than the Canon 5D Mark II), when you're in video shooting mode, you can lock the exposure by holding down the AE Lock/FE Lock button, at the top right of the back of the camera, to keep the exposure from constantly changing as you pan or move the camera. In addition, if you have the Canon 5D Mark II, thanks to a recent firmware update, you can also manually control the exposure by switching to manual mode. This allows you to manually adjust the exposure controls, such as ISO, aperture, and shutter speed, while shooting video.

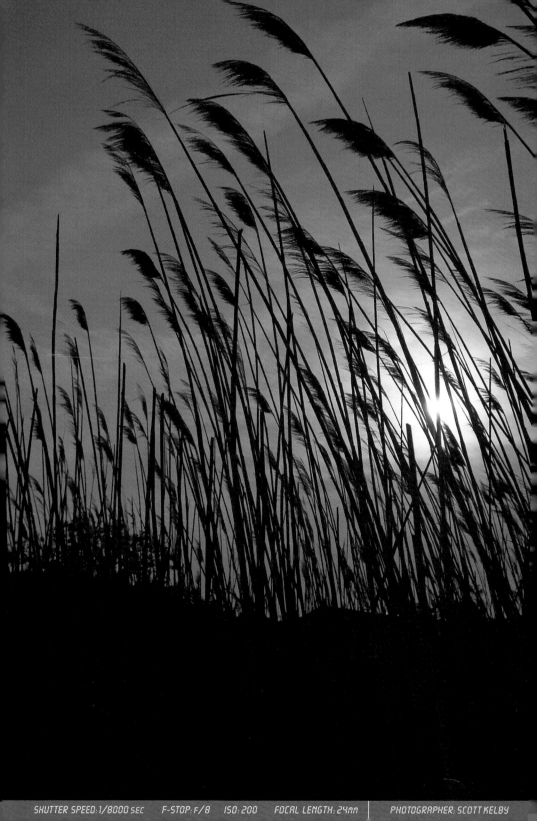

Chapter Nine

Avoiding Problems Like a Pro

How to Sidestep Those Things That Drive You Crazy

Today's digital cameras are amazingly sophisticated devices, and if you take a moment to really think about it, you're holding in your hands a lens, a shutter mechanism, a color TV monitor, and a computer. That's right, there actually is a computer inside every single digital camera. That's what those menus on the back are for—you're navigating the camera's software and turning on/off specific features, just like you do on your computer at work or at home. You're setting the preferences for how your computer works. So, at this point, you're not really taking a photo, you're tweaking your software to get a specific desired result. When you press the shutter button, it sends a signal to the software to briefly let some amount of light into the computer-controlled sensor, and that amount is determined through a mathematical calculation performed by (that's right) your onboard computer. So, is it any wonder that occasionally we make a mistake with this handheld computer, and a photo doesn't look how we wanted it to? No, it's not. So, technically, when the photo doesn't look the way we want it to, it's not our fault—it's that darn computer. Well, that's what this chapter is all about. Blame. You'll learn how to quickly and easily redirect the blame for any bad shot back to how the software behaved in your camera, and you'll be able to do it in such a convincing and logical way that there's no way you could ever be held personally responsible for taking any photo that is not literally Ansel Adams quality. Underexposed? "That stupid software!" Out of focus? "Darn autofocus got me again!" Took a shot of your foot as you were walking? "It fired without me pressing the button!" See? It's easier than you'd think. Let's try a few more: You hear, "Gee, the color looks off." You reply, "My stupid LCD isn't color balanced." (Oooh, good one!)

Can You Trust Your Camera's LCD Monitor?

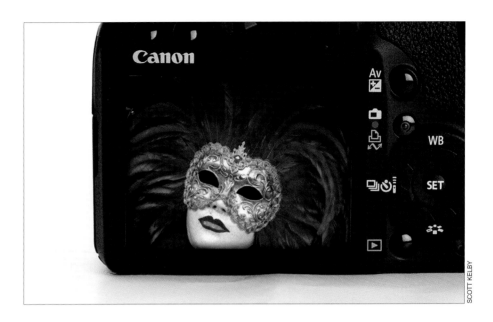

SCOTT KELBY

You read a lot online about not being able to really trust what you see on the LCD screen on the back of your camera. Some of that is old outdated information, some of it depends on camera settings (which we'll cover in just a minute), and some of it is true. Here are my thoughts on it: If you shoot in JPEG mode using one of today's newer dSLR cameras (and the more expensive the camera, usually the better quality the LCD monitor), what you're seeing on the monitor is a JPEG preview, and it's pretty close to what you'll actually see when you open the photo on your computer (or get prints made). However, if you shoot in RAW mode, you're not seeing a preview of the RAW photo—you're seeing a preview of the JPEG image, and the JPEG image usually looks better than an unedited RAW photo. That's because JPEG images have been "processed" inside your camera, and they have sharpening applied, color correction, contrast, and basically your camera tries to make JPEGs look really good. But when you shoot in RAW, you're telling your camera, "Turn all that in-camera, make-it-look-good stuff off, and just give me the raw, untouched file, and then I'll do all that sharpening, color correction, and contrast stuff myself in Photoshop, or Lightroom, or whatever." However, you're still seeing that processed JPEG preview on your camera, so if you shoot in RAW mode, don't be startled when what you see on your computer doesn't look nearly as good as it did on the back of your camera. I'm not telling you on any level not to shoot in RAW mode, I'm just letting you know how what you see on your LCD relates to what you're going to see on your computer. Now ya know.

Resetting Your Camera to the Factory Defaults

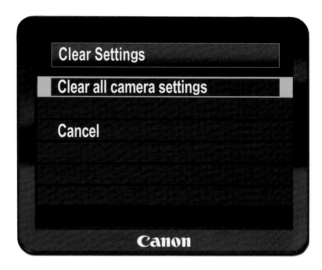

If you've tweaked and played around with the menus in your camera and you feel like you've totally messed something up, and you just wish everything was back like it was when you bought the camera, then you'll be happy to learn that most cameras have a "return to default" setting that puts all the customizable settings back to their original factory-default settings. I use this when it just seems like my camera is all whacked out for some reason, and resetting to the defaults usually snaps it right out of its insanity. The only downside of doing this is when it returns to the defaults, any of the settings you changed in your camera are erased, too, so you have to go back and customize whatever settings you had customized again (which is why it helps to write those little changes down—that way you won't forget what your settings were). Anyway, here's how it's done: On a Canon camera, you press the Menu button, then go to the Set-Up 3 menu, and choose Clear Settings. Now choose Clear All Camera Settings and then select OK. If you're using a Nikon camera, press-and-hold the Qual (Quality) button and the +/– (Exposure Compensation button) down for more than two seconds, or you can press the Menu button, go to the Shooting menu, and choose Reset Shooting Menu, then go to the Custom Setting menu, and choose Reset Custom Settings. Doesn't matter which way you do it, it'll reset the camera to the factory fresh settings.

Instant JPEG From RAW

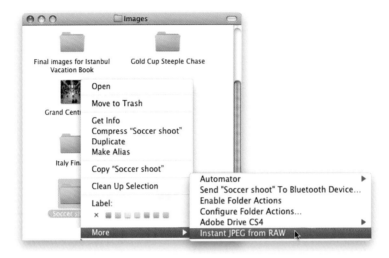

Most dSLRs these days will let you shoot RAW, or JPEG, and usually Raw + JPEG, which means it writes two separate files to your memory card—one is the untouched RAW file, and the other is a processed JPEG file. This is a big advantage for anyone who needs to quickly send a JPEG file to a client (like a pro sports photographer who needs to email shots to the magazine or wire service while the event is still going on. RAW files are much larger in file size, so they're a somewhat impractical for email, some clients don't have the software to read RAW files, and the files are unprocessed, unsharpened, and uncorrected, so having an already processed, compressed JPEG makes sense for some shooters). The downside is it takes up a lot more room on your memory card, and now you have two versions of every photo. Now, if you're one of those folks who shoots in Raw + JPEG, have I got a tip for you! Michael Tapes at RawWorkflow.com (the guy who makes the popular WhiBal white balance tool) created a free downloadable software utility that extracts the JPEG preview that's already embedded in every RAW image, and it does it incredibly, ludicrously (if that's even a word) fast! All you do is download the utility from www.rawworkflow.com and run the installer. Then, click on a folder of RAW photos, Control-click (PC: Right-click) on that folder, and choose Instant JPEG from RAW from the contextual menu that appears. You'll get to choose what size you'd like your JPEG (in case you need a smaller size for uploading to a website), and then click Extract and, literally in just seconds, it extracts those JPEGs for you and puts them in their own folder. I use this all the time, and I love it!

When to Shoot JPEG; When to Shoot RAW

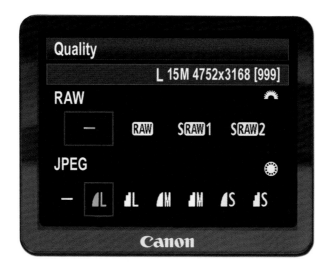

I get asked on a regular basis, "When should I shoot in RAW and when should I shoot in JPEG mode?" This is one sticky question, because some photographers are so fanati-cal about shooting in RAW that there's no reason you could ever give them that makes sense not to shoot in RAW. If the photo you're going to take is of your wrecked car, and it's only going to be 3x4" in size, and the only person who would ever possibly see it is the insurance adjuster in a different state processing your repair claim, they would still shoot it in RAW. So, for those people (you know who you are), I'm going to save myself a lot of angry letters (not all, mind you, but a few), and state categorically that you should shoot all photos, no matter what the final intended use, in RAW format. There, I said it. It's been documented. Now, that being said, I've heard of some photographers who don't post-process their images—meaning they don't open the photos in Photoshop, or Ele-ments, or Lightroom, or Capture, or whatever—they just take the shots, and then either put them on the Web, or put them on disc, or print them out as is. So, if you are one of those people who are pretty happy with how their photos look right out of the camera, and you do very little, if any, editing in a photo software application, and you enjoy fit-ting thousands of photos on a 4-GB memory card (rather than a few hundred), and you enjoy not having the hard drive on your laptop crammed full all the time, I guess in that situation, it's okay to shoot in JPEG Fine mode. Just don't ever tell anyone. Also, two other groups of people who often shoot in JPEG mode are pro sports photographers (who shoot thousands of shots per event), and many pro wedding photographers, as well, but hey—I'm not telling you it's okay (wink, wink).

Built-In Sensor Cleaning

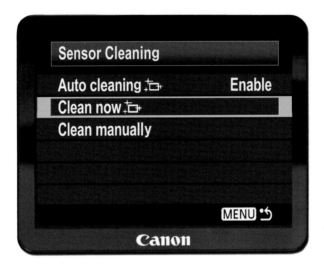

The sensor on your digital camera collects dust like…like…well, like something that really collects a lot of dust (like that film camera up in your closet). The sensors in today's cameras are magnetized, and each time you change lenses, you're screwing a piece of metal into a metal mount, and not surprisingly, tiny metal shavings appear, and those can get sucked down onto your sensor, and before you know it, you've got tiny spots and specks on your sensor, which means you now have tiny spots and specks on every photo you're about to take. That's why we have to do our best to keep our sensors clean, and that's why more and more of the newer digital cameras now have built-in sensor cleaning capabilities. This basically demagnetizes your sensor for a moment to shake the sensor dust off, and it does a decent job. Not a great job, an okay job (it doesn't replace having your sensor fully cleaned), but if your camera has it built-in, you might as well use it. For example, on a Canon camera like the 50D, if you turn the power switch to the On higher position, this turns on the auto sensor cleaning feature, and it shakes the dust off your sensor right then and there. It cleans the sensor when it shuts down, too. With the power switch in the On position, you can also go to the Set-Up 2 menu, choose Sensor Cleaning, and then choose Clean Now. If you have a Nikon camera (like a D300), press the Menu button, go to the Setup menu, and choose Clean Image Sensor. In the next menu, choose Clean Now, and your sensor will be cleaned. If you want it to automatically clean the sensor each time you turn on the camera, choose Clean at Startup/Shutdown.

Shortcut for Formatting Your Memory Card

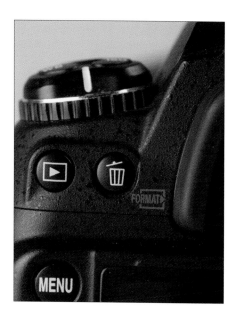
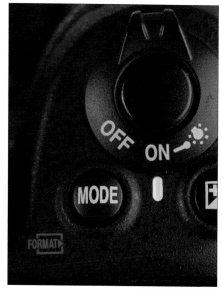

Many dSLRs have a shortcut which lets you quickly reformat (erase all your images on) your memory card without having to dig through all the menus on the back of the camera. On a Nikon, the shortcut actually appears in red beside the two buttons you need to hold down to reformat (you hold the Delete [trash can] button and the Mode button down together for two or three seconds, until you see the word "For" flashing in the LCD info window on top of the camera. Once "For" is flashing, release those buttons and press them again just once, and your card will format). On a Canon, there isn't a shortcut, but you can go under the Set-Up 1 menu, select Format, and then press the Set button. Select OK and your card will be formatted.

Don't Go Out Shooting with Just One Memory Card

If you shoot with just one memory card, it's going to catch up with you. Your card's going to be full, or you're going to have to wind up formatting the card without having two backups (or you'll have to stop shooting for the day), which is why you've got to have at least a second, if not a third, memory card with you on every shoot. I just checked and a 4-GB memory card is going for as little as $18.95. You can also find lots of cards with manufacturer's rebates (I recently bought a number of 8-GB memory cards for $69 with a $69 mail-in rebate. I kid you not. That's right—free cards. It happens).

Make Sure You Have the Latest Firmware

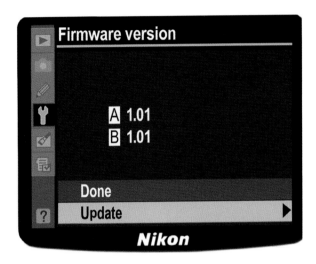

One huge advantage of having the brains of today's digital cameras run by software is that the camera manufacturer can release updates to your camera, which can range from fixing problems in the camera (bugs) to adding new features. These free camera updates are called "firmware" updates and you download them directly from the manufacturer's website. Once an update is downloaded, you just connect your camera to your computer (using that little USB cable that came with your camera), and run the firmware updater software (which usually has some simple instructions with it), and it updates your camera (by the way, it's not just cameras that get firmware updates—off-camera flash units can get them, too). The good news is they don't issue firmware updates very often—maybe only two or three times in the life of a camera, so this isn't something you'll have to be checking every week, but it doesn't hurt to stop by Google.com every once in a while and type in your camera's name plus firmware (so your search would be "Canon 50D" + "Firmware update" or "Nikon D700" + "Firmware update"), and you'll find a direct link to download the update from the manufacturer. Once you find the update online, check to see if the one available online is a higher number than the one currently installed on your camera (for example, on Nikon or Canon cameras, you go under the Setup menu and choose Firmware Version, and it will show you the version of your currently installed firmware [like version 1.01]). So, if you see that a more recent firmware update has been released (like firmware version 1.02 [or higher]), you'll want to download and install that firmware.

Don't Get Burned by Shooting Without a Memory Card

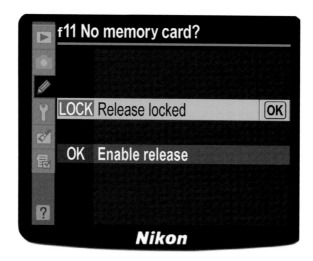

When camera manufacturers ship their cameras to camera stores, they want the sales people at the camera store to be able to open a camera box and hand the customer the camera to take a few shots and see how the camera feels (after all, how a camera feels in your hands is very important). So, at the factory, they set the camera up so you can take shots without actually having a memory card in the camera. The shutter fires just like usual, and you see the picture appear on the LCD on the back of the camera, just like always, except those photos vanish into thin air after, because they're not saved to a memory card. This is one thing you usually learn about the hard way. Well, at least I did when I did a photo shoot in a studio—I shot for 35 minutes—and when I popped the door on my camera open to back up my photos, I was shocked to find out there was no memory card, even though I had been looking at some of the shots on the camera's LCD monitor. Those shots were gone forever, so the first thing I do with any new camera is turn the memory card lock on, so it won't even take a shot without a memory card in the camera. On Canon cameras, go to the Shooting menu and choose Shoot Without Card, then set this function to Off. On Nikon cameras, go under the Custom Setting menu and choose No Memory Card. Change the setting from Enable Release to Release Locked. Now, the camera's shutter release will be locked, and it won't take a shot unless a memory card is in the camera.

You Need to Copyright Your Photos

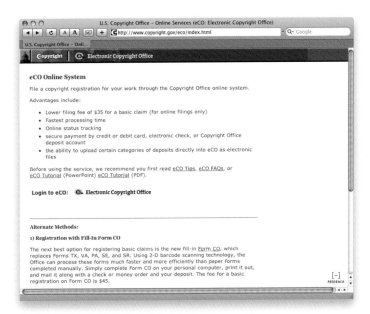

With so many of us posting our images on the Web, you've got to protect yourself (and your images) by legally copyrighting your work. Luckily, the process (at least in the U.S.) is all now Web-based, so it's never been faster, easier, or more affordable than it is today. What copyrighting does is to legally define who owns the photo, and even though, technically, there is some very limited amount of protection afforded simply by the fact that you took the shot, if someone takes your photo off the Web and uses it in their brochure, or website, or print ad, etc., without actually having registered your work as copyrighted with the U.S. Copyright office, your chances of winning a judgment in court against the "photo thief" are virtually nil. Because this process has become so quick, easy, and inexpensive, there's no reason not to add this process as part of your photo workflow. To register your work online in the U.S., start by going to www.copyright.gov/eco/index.html (it only costs $35, and you can register literally thousands of photos at a time for that same fee). By the way, make sure you read the tip below.

Watch These Free, Short, Absolutely Fascinating Videos on Copyright

I did a series of video interviews with intellectual property attorney and noted photography copyright expert Ed Greenburg, and followed up with interviews with photographer rights advocate Jack Resnicki, in July 2008. These videos have been a huge hit with photographers, and I invite you to watch them on my blog: www.scottkelby.com. Once you're there, search for copyright and you'll find the videos.

Back Up Twice Before Formatting

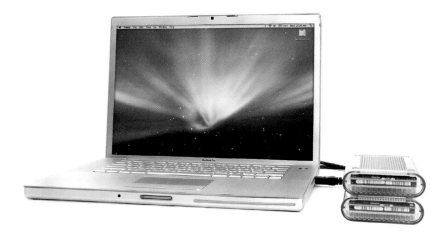

There's a rule a lot of photographers (well, paranoid photographers anyway, like me) follow, and that is: we don't erase our memory cards until we absolutely know that we have two copies of our photos elsewhere. For example, when you download your photos to your computer, that's only one copy, and you shouldn't format your memory card with just this one copy (because when your hard drive crashes one day [notice that I said "when"] all those photos are gone forever). Now, once you back up those photos from your computer to a second drive (a backup hard drive), then you'll have two copies—one set on your computer and one set on your backup drive—and then it's safe to format (erase) your memory card and keep shooting with that card. Without two backups, it's just a matter of time before those photos are gone forever (I could tell you the saddest stories of people who have written me who have lost every photo of their kids for the past eight or 10 years, because they had them on their computer, and their computer died. I wish it was just one story, but I've got dozens and dozens).

My Personal Photo Backup Strategy

I wrote about my entire photography backup and archiving strategy in a very detailed article on my blog at www.scottkelby.com/blog/2008/archives/1410, and if you're paranoid about losing all your photos (and you should be), it's worth a read.

How You Press the Shutter Button Matters!

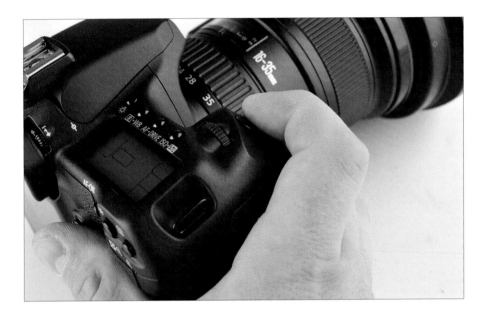

Want another tip for getting sharper images? Start gently squeezing the shutter button, rather than just pressing it. Actually, for the least vibration possible, you should kind of roll your finger over the shutter button from back to front. By doing this gentle pressing of the shutter button, you'll wind up with sharper photos every time.

Tuck in Your Elbows for Sharper Shots

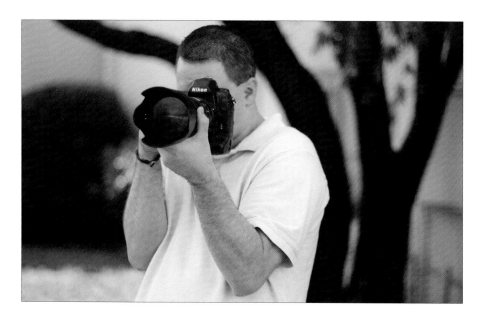

Another technique for getting sharper photos when hand-holding your camera is to steady the camera by holding it with your elbows tucked in toward your body. This helps anchor the camera to your body, keeping it steadier, and giving you sharper photos. This is an easier change to make than you'd think, and once you see the results, you'll be glad you did it.

Don't Let the Small Screen Fool You!

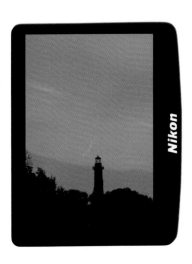
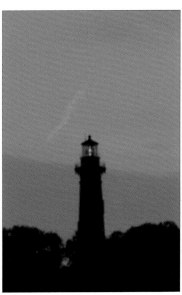

SCOTT KELBY

If you've ever taken a shot that looked great on your camera, only to open it later on your computer to find out that your killer shot was incredibly blurry, don't feel bad—everything looks sharp on a tiny 2.5" or 3" LCD screen, and every photographer has been burned by this (well, every photographer I know anyway). That's why it's so critical to check the sharpness right then and there—out in the field—while you still have a chance to reshoot the shot. When you see a shot that looks really great on the LCD, stop right there and make sure it's sharp by zooming in tight and checking the focus. Just press the Zoom In (on a Nikon) or Magnify (on a Canon) button on the back of the camera to zoom in. Once zoomed in, you move to view different parts of your zoomed-in photo using the multi selector (on a Nikon) or the multi-controller (on a Canon) on the back of the camera. Once you're done checking the sharpness, press the Zoom In (magnifying glass) button again (on a Nikon) or the Reduce button (on a Canon) to zoom back out. Keep your surprises to a minimum by checking the sharpness now, in camera, before it's too late.

Avoiding the Memory Card Moment of Doubt

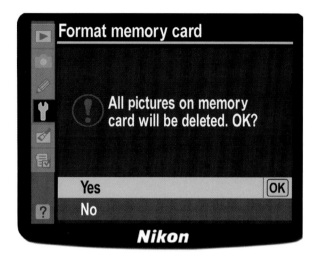

If you use more than one memory card (and I highly recommend that you do—see the tip at the bottom of page 197), you'll have experienced that "moment of doubt" when you go reaching for your second memory card, and you ask yourself, "What's on this card? Have I downloaded these? Is it okay to erase it?" I've had it happen to me more than once, but here's a way to avoid this moment of doubt altogether. Once you've download-ed the images to your computer, and then backed them up to a second hard drive (CDs and DVDs are a little too risky), right then and there, format your memory card. That way, if you see a memory card in your memory card case, you know it's formatted and ready to go, and that the images that were once on there are now safely backed up twice.

Shoot Multiple Shots in Low-Light Situations

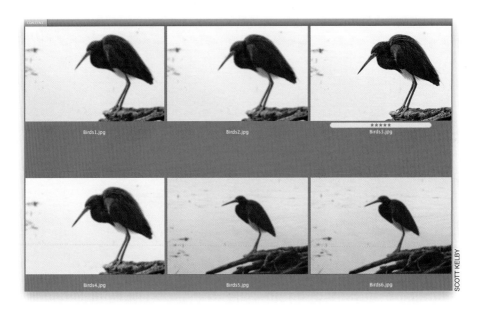

SCOTT KELBY

If you're in a situation where you're having to shoot in low light without a tripod (if your shutter speed gets under 1/60 of second, there's a pretty good chance your photo will be somewhat blurry if you're hand-holding), and you don't want to raise your ISO because your photo will get too noisy, here's a trick you can try that will usually get a sharp photo: shoot multiple shots in Burst or High-Speed Continuous mode. Chances are, if you take three or four shots in a quick burst, at least one of those shots will be in focus. I've done this numerous times and I'm always amazed at the results. You'll see a blurry one, blurry one, then all of a sudden there's a nice crisp shot (as shown here with the five-star image labeled yellow), and then right back to blurry. So, next time you're in one of those situations, crank off a few right in a row, and keep your fingers crossed that at least one of those will be in focus (hey, it's better than the alternative).

The High-Speed Memory Card Myth

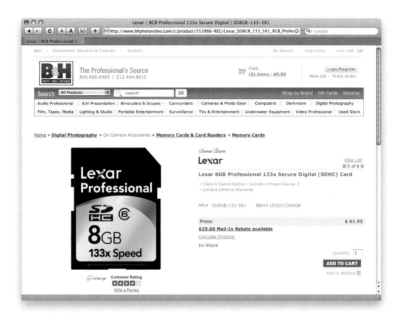

If you upgrade to the latest high-speed Compact Flash or SD memory cards, is it going to really make a difference? Well, honestly, for most folks—probably not. These more expensive high-speed cards are designed for people like serious sports photographers, with higher-end dSLRs, who need to shoot long, continuous bursts of images. The reason high-speed cards matter to them is that they need any images temporarily stored in their camera's built-in memory buffer to be written to the memory card as quickly as possible to free that buffer for their next continuous burst of shots. If you're reading this and thinking, "I never shoot that many shots at once," then there's good news—you don't really need one of those expensive high-speed cards. This is good news, because regular-speed cards are much less expensive. For example, I just looked up what a regular 8-GB SD Lexar memory card costs at B&H Photo. It was $9.99. The 133x higher-speed 8-GB card sells for $61.95, but it did come with a mail-in rebate of $25 (however, retail statistics show only a very small percentage of consumers ever actually mail in these rebates, which is why mail-in rebates are so popular), but even with that, it's still $36.95—more than 3.5 times as much as the regular-speed card. So, why pay the difference if you won't experience a difference, eh?

Do This Before You Close Your Camera Bag

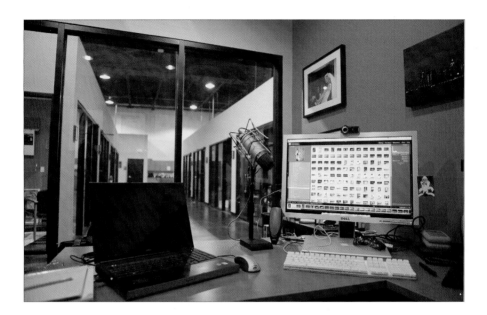

My friend Janine Smith shared this tip with me last year, and ever since she did, I've been using it and it's saved my bacon more than once. When you're packing your camera bag for a shoot, before you close the bag, pick up the camera and take a quick shot of anything. This will tell you instantly if you have a memory card with you, whether your battery is charged, and whether your camera is in basic working order. You don't want to learn about any of these problems once you're on location (or on vacation). You'd rather know now, while you still have time to grab a memory card, charge your battery, or fix a potential problem.

Why You Should Download Your User Manual

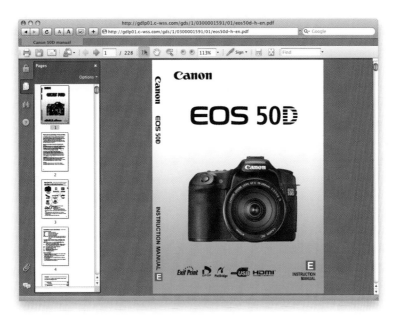

One of the biggest problems with camera user manuals is quickly finding what you're looking for. That's why I always download the free PDF electronic version of the user manual from the manufacturer's website, because the PDF versions have a search feature, and you can find what you're looking for in five seconds, rather than five minutes (of course, it's only five minutes if you're lucky. I've spent much more time looking for certain features). Once you use the free PDF version of the manual, you'll only reach for the printed manual in an emergency situation, when you're out in the field and you don't mind hauling the user manual around with you. By the way, I download the manuals for all my gear—flashes, cameras, wireless triggers, you name it. They're so small in file size, and so handy, there's no reason not to.

Where to Find Those Downloadable Manuals

If you're a Nikon user in the U.S., go to www.nikonusa.com/Service-And-Support/Download-Center.page, and if you're a Canon user in the U.S., go to www.usa.canon.com, click on the Download link in the menu bar across the top, and choose Consumer.

The Photoshop Trick for Finding Dust Spots

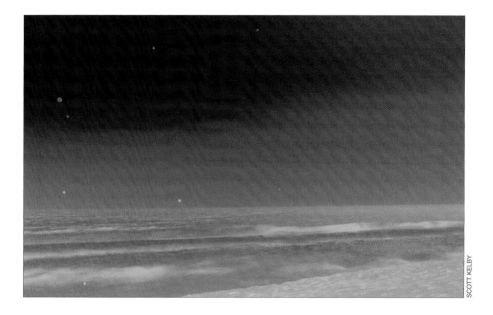

SCOTT KELBY

If you want to do a quick test to see if you've got "junk" on your camera's sensor, try this: aim at something like a solid gray wall, or a gray, cloudless sky, and take a shot. Import this photo into your computer, open it in Photoshop, and then press Command-I (PC: Ctrl-I). This inverts your photo, and any spots, specks, dust, or junk will stick out like a sore thumb, and you'll know right then if you need to clean your camera's sensor (by the way, although you can buy sensor cleaning kits, and cleaning your sensor is surprisingly easy, some folks just don't feel comfortable digging around inside their camera body, and in that case, you should stop by your local camera store and have one of their techs do a quick cleaning for you. They'll charge you a few bucks for it, but it beats having spots on all your shots). Make sure you do this before a big trip. (See page 196 for a tip on using your camera's built-in sensor cleaner.)

Shooting in Bad Weather

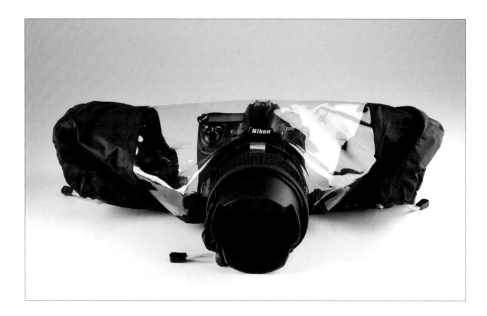

Sometimes the best images come from the worst weather, but if you're going to be shooting in this type of weather, you need to take a few precautions for your gear. Some cameras, like Nikon's D300, D700, and D3 line, have weather-sealed bodies that help keep moisture out, but your best bet is to buy rain covers for your gear that still allow you to hold your camera and operate the zooms on your lenses, while keeping the electronics inside your camera nice and dry. The set I use is the KT E-702 Elements Cover made by Kata (www.kata-bags.com), and it's got special sleeves on the side so you can reach inside the cover and adjust your camera settings and lens zoom. I don't have to use this often, but when I do, it's great not having to worry about my gear getting toasted. If you get caught in an unexpected rain situation, try using the shower cap from your hotel room to cover the entire back of your camera body (so just the lens sticks out).

What to Do When You Don't Have Protective Gear

If you get caught in the rain and don't have protective gear (hey, it happens), when you get back to a dry place, try patting dry the outside of your gear with a cleaning cloth, or a dry towel if a cleaning cloth isn't handy. Don't wipe it, or you risk moving water into places you don't want it, so just carefully pat it dry. I've heard of photographers using a blow dryer set on low to help dry things off, but luckily I haven't had to test that one out. Also, leave your camera off until the camera has had plenty of time to dry the inside on its own.

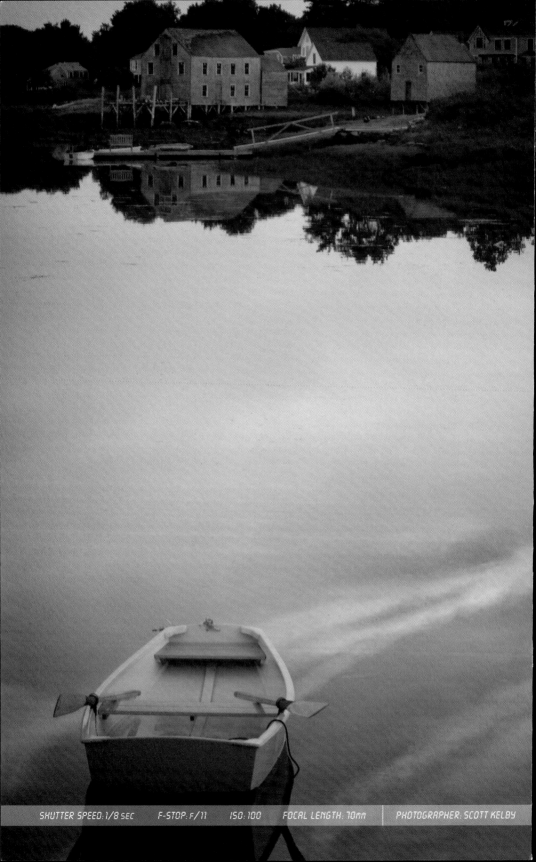

Chapter Ten

Yet Even More Photo Recipes to Help You Get "The Shot"

The Simple Ingredients to Make It All Come Together

Have you ever looked at a photo and thought, "I wonder how you get a shot like that?" Maybe it was a studio shot, or one taken out on location, and you're wondering where the light was positioned, or maybe if there was even a light at all. Maybe you could figure out that there was a flash of some sort used, but maybe you didn't know which type of softbox was used, or if there was more than one light. Has that ever happened to you? No? Really? Rats! That's going to make this chapter a hard sell for you, because like its two predecessors in volumes 1 and 2, this is more of those types of things, but if you're not into that, then we'll have to come up with a way to give this chapter real value for you. Wait…wait…I've got it! Let's make it a "photo treasure hunt." Yeah, I'll give you objects, and you look through the images in this chapter (being careful not to actually read any of the detailed step-by-step instructions on how to recreate those looks yourself), and then you find them. Now, once you find all these items, then go to the website www.ohyouhavetobekiddingme.com, and there you'll find a form with a broken link where you can fill in which page you found each object on, and then in a month or so, I'll forget to go to that site to choose a winner (from all the entries that didn't get submitted), and that lucky person (probably you, by the way) will win a free copy of one of my books (probably this book), and we'll ship that copy directly to you (probably sometime next year), but by then you'll have moved to a new address (you're probably running from the law), and delivery will be refused by the current occupant (your ex), and then I'll get the book back and send it to the next winner on the list (probably your parole officer). Or you could just read the chapter and see what you think. Really, it's your call.

The Recipe for Getting This Type of Shot

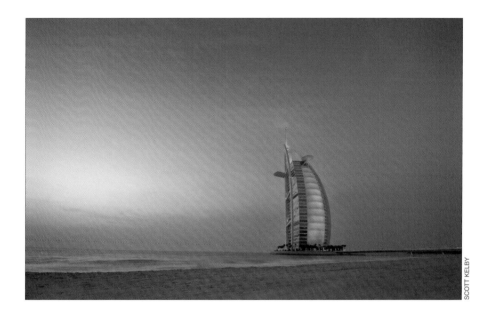

SCOTT KELBY

Characteristics of this type of shot: A sweeping shot that's both a landscape and travel shot in one, and with lots of detail all the way through and a clear focus on the hotel, there's no doubt what the subject is. (The location is the Burj Al Arab hotel, Dubai, UAE.)

(1) You need to use a very-wide-angle lens to capture this type of expanse. This was shot at 14mm with a 14–24mm wide-angle zoom lens on a full-frame camera, which makes the lens even wider than usual.

(2) To capture all the detail front to back, shoot in aperture priority (Av) mode, and choose the highest number f-stop you can (this was shot at f/22, which keeps every-thing in focus from front to back).

(3) This was taken right around sunset, so the light is low, which means you absolutely need to shoot on a tripod to keep the shot sharp and in focus. It also means the light is going to be gorgeous (even though the sun is tucked behind the clouds, the clouds are still great because they hold a lot of the color).

(4) To eliminate any camera shake, you can either shoot with a cable release or, at the very least, use the camera's built-in self-timer to take the shot, so your finger isn't even touching the camera when the shot is taken.

The Recipe for Getting This Type of Shot

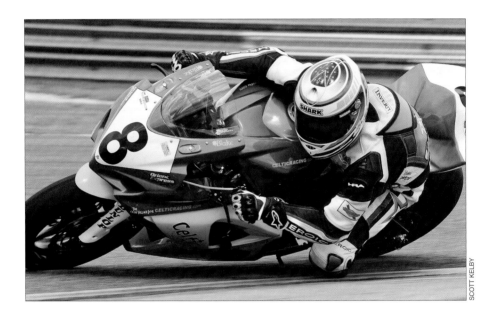

SCOTT KELBY

Characteristics of this type of shot: You're in really tight, which pulls you into the action, and the rotation of the wheels gives you a sense of movement, but without blurring the rest of the image.

(1) To get in really close like this, you need a long lens (this was taken with a 200mm lens with a 1.4x teleconverter to get in even closer).

(2) The key to this shot is finding a shutter speed that freezes the action enough for the bike and rider to remain sharp, yet keep some blur in the wheels, so it doesn't look like the bike is standing still. You can freeze most sports shots at 1/1000 of a second, so to see some wheel-spin, you know right off the bat it has to be slower than 1/1000. This was taken at 1/400 of a second.

(3) If you're shooting at a slow shutter speed like this (well, 1/400 of a second is slow for sports anyway), you'll need to pan (follow) along with the bike to keep the bike and rider sharp. You won't be shooting on a tripod, so keep your camera steady when panning (if you're using a long enough lens, you can try using a monopod).

(4) When panning like this, you need to be shooting in high-speed continuous (burst) mode to increase your chances of getting a sharp shot.

The Recipe for Getting This Type of Shot

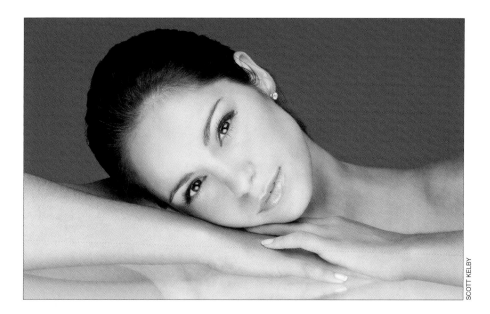

SCOTT KELBY

Characteristics of this type of shot: A "beauty-style" shot with soft, full lighting that wraps around your subject and gives you bright, flat, almost shadowless light.

(1) There are two keys to a beauty-style shot like this: The first is to have the subject put her hair back into a ponytail and hide as much of that behind her head as possible, leaving the face open and clean. The second is the lighting, which bathes the subject in light and gives the image the clean beauty look.

(2) There are just two lights used for this look: the main light is a beauty dish that's directly in front of the subject, but up about two feet above her face, aiming down at her at a 45° angle. The other light is under the plexiglass, aiming up at her at a 45° angle (this is sometimes called "clamshell" lighting, because it looks like you're shooting in between an open clamshell). Position the camera height right at her eye level.

(3) To keep everything in focus, from front to back, you'll need to use an f-stop that holds details, like f/11, and a long enough lens (like a 200mm) to give nice perspective.

(4) She's leaning on the same clear piece of plexiglass that I talked about in the product photography chapter (Chapter 4), which is held up by two people assisting in the studio. The background is a gray seamless paper background.

The Recipe for Getting This Type of Shot

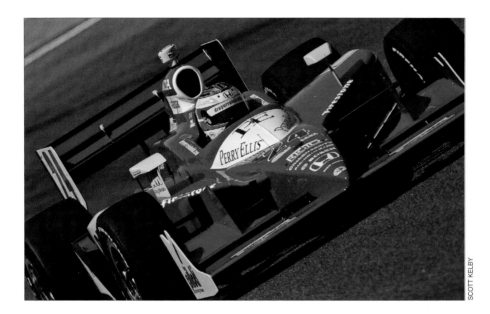

SCOTT KELBY

Characteristics of this type of shot: A tight-in shot, giving you an up-close view you don't usually see, and the shot has a lot of energy and vivid color.

(1) The key to this shot is using a very long lens (in this case, a 400mm lens) to get you really in tight to the action.

(2) Because you're shooting in direct sunlight during the middle of the day, getting a shutter speed greater than 1/1000 of a second won't be a problem at all (in fact, this was shot at 1/4000 of a second, which freezes everything).

(3) Because the car is coming almost straight at your shooting position, you hardly see the wheels like you do with a side or three-quarter view of the car, so you don't have to be as concerned about using a slow shutter speed to have the wheels blurred to show motion. Because of that, you can shoot with a much higher shutter speed and create a really crisp image.

(4) One thing that greatly adds to the energy of the shot is tilting the camera 45° to one side—a very popular angle for motorsports shots.

(5) You'll want to use a monopod to steady a lens 300mm or longer.

The Recipe for Getting This Type of Shot

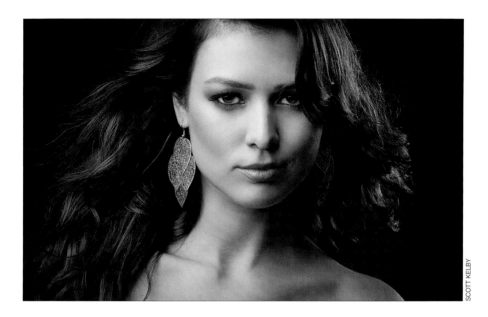

SCOTT KELBY

Characteristics of this type of shot: Dramatic lighting that doesn't evenly light the subject. Having a subject with dark hair on a dark background adds to the drama.

(1) To get this type of shot, you need just two lights: the main light is a large softbox positioned to the left (from our view) and slightly in front of the subject, but very close to the subject to create very soft light. The key is to keep this large softbox mostly to the side of the subject, so the light doesn't fully light her entire face—you want those shadows on the right side of her face to add drama. Keep the power on the main light down about as low as it will go, since it will be so close to the subject.

(2) The second light is a strip bank (a tall, thin softbox) positioned behind your subject on the right side (from our view), lighting her hair and shoulders (it's at a 45° angle about eight feet behind her to the right). The reason the light doesn't spill over every-where is that there's a fabric grid over the strip bank (I talked about these in volume 2).

(3) This was shot with the subject on a black seamless paper background. No reflector is necessary and no tripod is necessary (the flash will freeze your subject). It was taken at f/8 to keep everything from front to back in focus.

(4) To get a little movement in her hair, just add a fan (any old fan will do).

The Recipe for Getting This Type of Shot

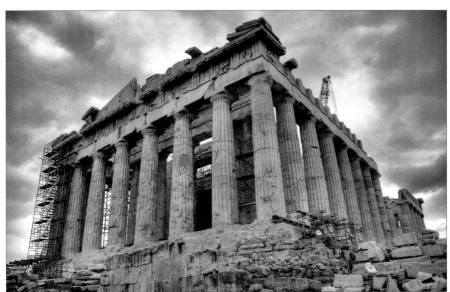

SCOTT KELBY

Characteristics of this type of shot: Lots of detail throughout the shot, including both highlight and shadow areas, and a surreal look in the sky.

(1) The key to this shot is shooting bracketed in your camera, so that later you can combine the bracketed shots into an HDR image using Photoshop and/or Photomatix Pro.
(2) This was taken in the middle of the day, in direct sunlight (it wasn't as cloudy as it appears—the clouds are enhanced by the HDR effect), so there's enough light to use an f-stop of f/11 or higher, which keeps as much of the image in focus as possible from front to back. Set your camera to three- or five-image bracketing (see page 117 for how to do that).
(3) To take all this in, you'll need a wide-angle lens (I used an 18–200mm lens, so I shot this at 18mm for the widest view possible).
(4) Although I didn't use a tripod for this particular shot (I didn't have one with me), HDR shots work best when you can shoot on a tripod (although, obviously, you can get away with hand-holding an HDR shot if you have Photoshop CS3 or CS4, and can use the Auto-Align Layers feature to perfectly align the shots later, before you create the HDR image). I created a video just for you to show how to combine your bracketed shots into an HDR image like you see above. The link to it is on page 118.

The Recipe for Getting This Type of Shot

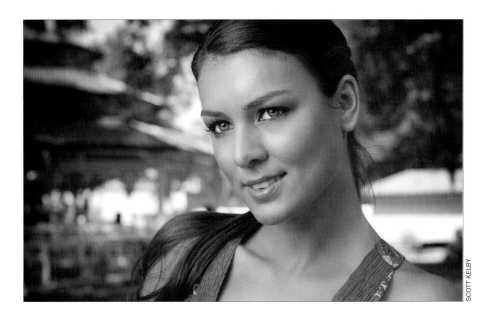

SCOTT KELBY

Characteristics of this type of shot: An outdoor portrait, taken at midday, with soft directional lighting (the opposite of what you'd get at midday).

(1) The first step is to get your subject out of the direct sunlight. If you look at the setup shot on page 30, the subject (above) is standing under a tree, but there's lots of light coming through the branches, so you'd have her move back a few feet, so there are no dapples of light falling on her—you want her completely in the shade.

(2) To light a shot like this, all you need is one single off-camera flash (in this case, a Nikon SB-800 flash) on a light stand, up high in front of her and to the left (from our view). You need something to soften the light—in this case, we used a Lastolite Ezybox (as seen back on page 7).

(3) To separate the subject from the background, you need to have the background blurry and out of focus, so you'll need to use a very low-numbered aperture. In this case, I used an f-stop of f/5.6 (the lower the number you use, the more out of focus the background will be).

(4) Set your flash at a very low power, so it blends in with the existing light. You don't need to shoot on a tripod, because the flash will freeze your subject.

The Recipe for Getting This Type of Shot

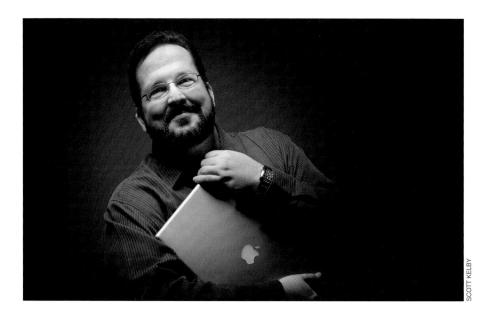

SCOTT KELBY

Characteristics of this type of shot: A dark, dramatic editorial-style shot.

(1) This is a simple one-light shot. It's a beauty dish (of all things) positioned directly above the subject's head, aiming straight down (like a street lamp).

(2) Because the light is aiming straight downward, some of the light is spilling onto the black seamless paper background, giving a little spotlight effect behind the subject.

(3) The subject is not a professional model, and didn't know what to do with his hands, so since he's kind of a Mac freak, we handed him a laptop. This is a great trick to use when your subject is uncomfortable in front of the camera—just hand them a prop, give them something to do, and then just capture the moment as they interact with the prop (which is what happened here, when he started jokingly hugging the laptop).

(4) The final key to this is having the light fall off, so his face is well lit, but then the light falls off as it moves down. This was done by placing a black flag (a 24x36" felt panel) just below the bottom edge of the beauty dish. That way, the light didn't spill too much onto his chest, and mostly concentrated on his face. This was shot with a 70–200mm f/2.8 lens (at 85mm) at f/6.3.

The Recipe for Getting This Type of Shot

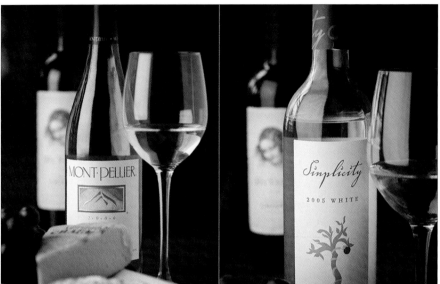

SCOTT KELBY

Characteristics of this type of shot: Soft daylight-looking light, with large, tall highlights in the bottles and glasses, and a very shallow depth of field.

(1) These shots are a mixture of natural light and continuous daylight fluorescent studio lighting. The natural daylight was coming from a window behind and to the left (from our view) of the wine bottles.

(2) The main light (lighting the front of the wine bottles) is a Westcott Spiderlite (not a strobe, but a continuous light) using daylight fluorescent bulbs with a 24x36" softbox attached to soften the light. The light is just off to the left of the wine bottle, and in really close (just outside the left side of the camera frame). To get that nice tall reflection, just rotate the softbox so it's tall (rather than a wide).

(3) Both lights (the natural window light and the Spiderlite continuous light) are on the left side of the frame, so to bounce some light back into the dark area on the right side of the bottles is a white foam core reflector (you can buy these at your local office supply store), and it's standing straight up, to the right of the wine bottles, just outside the frame.

(4) This is a product shot, so shoot it on a tripod (especially in lower light like this).

The Recipe for Getting This Type of Shot

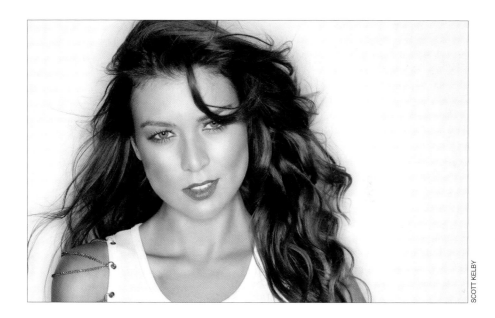

SCOTT KELBY

Characteristics of this type of shot: This is the bright, flat, shadowless look that's very popular right now in flash photography. However, with ring flash, you'll actually see a shadow halo outlining your subject, which is part of "the look."

(1) There's only one light—an AlienBees Ring Flash (seen on page 47), which is a circle of very small flashes, and your lens goes through the middle of this circle of flashes, so it's mounted right to the camera. You shoot from directly in front of your subject.
(2) Normally, you'd keep your subject about 10 feet away from the white seamless paper background, but to get that halo shadow behind her, you can reposition your subject so she's only around a foot or two from the background. That way, you can see the shadows created by the ring flash, but they're not too large.
(3) Since you're this close to the background, you don't need to light the background with a separate flash—the light from the ring flash is enough to light the background at the same time.
(4) A ring flash produces a harder light source than a strobe with a softbox, so to keep the shadows that outline your subject soft, make sure you shoot in close to your subject (this increases the relative size of your light source, which makes the light softer).

The Recipe for Getting This Type of Shot

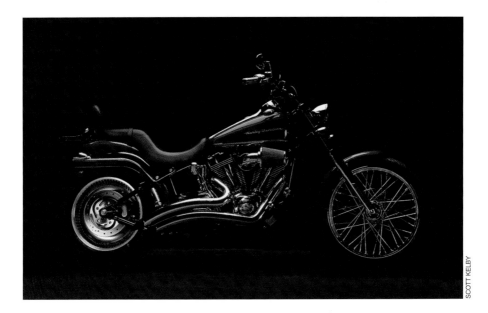

SCOTT KELBY

Characteristics of this type of shot: Dark, dramatic lighting that picks up the chrome and the lines of the bike.

(1) You only need one light to get a shot like this, but it has to be a big one (well, the strobe doesn't have to be big, but the softbox does—it has to almost be as long as the bike). Place the softbox directly over the motorcycle, on a large boom stand, aiming straight down at it.

(2) The reason you don't see the legs of the boom stand holding up the light is that I removed them using the Clone Stamp tool (found in Photoshop or Photoshop Elements). In the original, you could see part of the base of the rolling boom stand, and even part of the light stand itself, just to the right of the front tire.

(3) To keep the bike pretty sharp throughout, use an f-stop of at least f/8 or higher.

(4) This is essentially a product shot and since that's the case, you need to shoot it on a tripod to keep the image really sharp and crisp.

The Recipe for Getting This Type of Shot

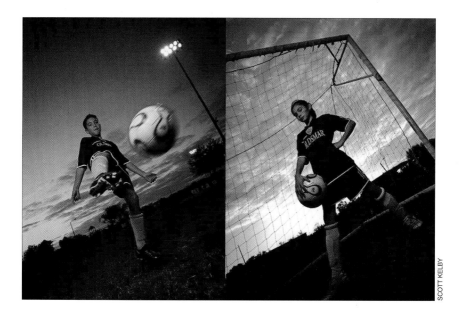

SCOTT KELBY

Characteristics of this type of shot: A great mix of sunset color and on-location flash, coupled with a shooting angle that makes these young kids look larger than life.

(1) There are two keys to the shot: The first being composition. To make the kids look big, you have to get down really low and shoot upward with a wide-angle lens (I used a 14–24mm ultra-wide-angle zoom on a full-frame camera). When I say to shoot really low, you actually need to be lying on the ground shooting upward to get this perspective. The other key to this shot is waiting until right around sunset to take it.

(2) The kids are lit using an off-camera flash (in this case, a Nikon SB-900 flash) mounted on a lightweight, portable light stand, with a small Ezybox softbox in front of it to soften and control the spill of the light. For both shots, the flash on the stand was on their right (from our view), just outside the frame.

(3) The key here is to switch to program mode, turn off the flash, aim at your subject, hold the shutter button halfway down, and then look to see the shutter speed and f-stop chosen by your camera. Then switch to manual mode, put in that f-stop and shutter speed, turn the flash on, and put the power really low—just enough to light your subject. Also, put an orange gel over the flash head, so the light from your flash doesn't look so white and artificial.

The Recipe for Getting This Type of Shot

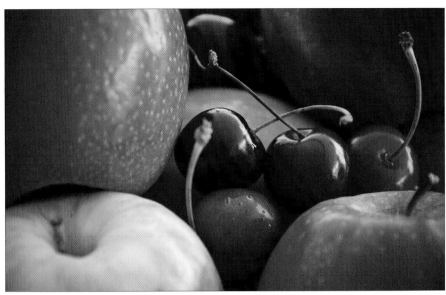

SCOTT KELBY

Characteristics of this type of shot: A cropped-in-tight shot with lots of detail, high-lights, and shadows.

(1) It's a natural-light shot—a bowl of fruit, on a table, in the shade. All you have to do here is position yourself (or rotate the bowl), so the light is coming from one side, giv-ing the photo depth and dimension.

(2) Shoot standing far back, and zoom all the way in to 200mm to get this tight compo-sition. The shot was taken with my favorite all-around travel lens, an 18–200mm lens.

(3) When you're shooting in open shade like this, there's no direct light, so you're going to have to shoot at the lowest number your lens will allow (in this case, f/5.6) to be able to hand-hold the shot and still keep it in focus. This will give you a somewhat shal-low depth of field (especially when you're zoomed-in tight like this, which is when the depth of field really kicks in). Notice how the apples in front are a bit out of focus, but the cherries are nice and sharp, and the apples behind the cherries are also out of focus. That's the f/5.6 at work for you. If I could have gone to a lower number f-stop (like f/4 or, ideally, f/2.8) the depth of field would have been even shallower.

(4) By shooting in aperture priority mode, all you do is choose the f-stop, and your camera will automatically choose the proper shutter speed for you.

The Recipe for Getting This Type of Shot

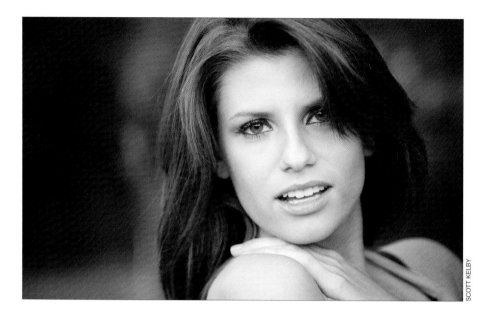

SCOTT KELBY

Characteristics of this type of shot: A soft, natural-light portrait where the subject has great separation from the background.

(1) There are four keys to this shot: The first is to shoot very late in the day (but before sunset). The sun is lower in the sky and the angle makes the shadows appear softer, and this late-day sun is generally a more flattering light.

(2) The second key is to position your subject so the sunlight is coming from one side. In this photo, the sunlight is coming from her left (from our view), and if you look at her hair, you'll see it's brighter on the left and more in the shadows on the right.

(3) The third key to this shot is to just make sure your subject is not in direct sunlight, but on the edge of a shady area (in this case, she's just below the thick branches of a tree high above). Because you're shooting in the shade, you'll have to increase the ISO a bit to make sure you have enough shutter speed (more than 1/60 of a second) to keep the image sharp if you're hand-holding your camera (this was taken at 800 ISO).

(4) To have such great separation between the subject and the background, you need a zoom lens so you can zoom in tight (here I'm zoomed in to 200mm), and you need the lowest number f-stop you can use (in this case, f/2.8 to get a nice shallow depth of field).

The Recipe for Getting This Type of Shot

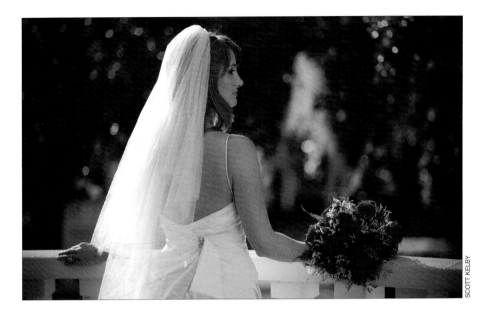

SCOTT KELBY

Characteristics of this type of shot: A bright backlight mixed with soft fill light, and a shallow depth of field to create separation of your subject from the background.

(1) One thing that gives the photo a dream-like quality is the very shallow depth of field, and you get that by using the smallest number f-stop (in this case, f/2.8), and by zooming in using a long lens (in this case, a 70–200mm lens, zoomed in to 150mm).

(2) To keep the sun from being harsh, you need to shoot a shot like this very late in the day (but at least one hour before sunset).

(3) The bride is backlit, with the sun behind her and to the left (from our view) light-ing the back of her veil. To keep her face from appearing in shadow, position a white reflector to the right of the bride's bouquet to bounce some of that sunlight back onto her face. White reflectors aren't all that powerful, so she doesn't look washed in light, because the bounced light looks pretty natural.

(4) The thing to keep an eye out for is blowing out (clipping) the highlights in her veil. If you have your highlight warning turned on, and you see her veil blinking (warn-ing you that the veil is blowing out), use your exposure compensation to lower the exposure by one-third of a stop, and take a test shot. If it's still blinking, lower it more, and test again, and so on.

The Recipe for Getting This Type of Shot

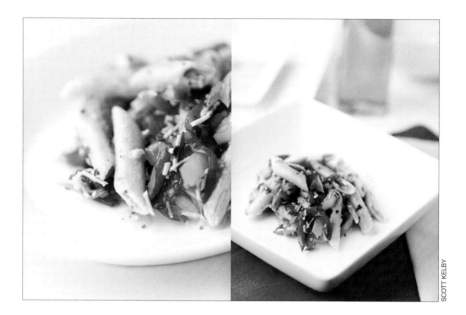

SCOTT KELBY

Characteristics of this type of shot: A bright, fresh look to the lighting, and a very shallow depth of field.

(1) The key to this type of shot is backlighting. Place the main (most powerful) light behind the food, and then use a lower-powered light in front.

(2) These shots were lit with a two Westcott Spiderlite daylight fluorescent lights (these are continuous lights—see page 88). The larger light is placed behind the food, on the left (from the camera view), and the second, smaller light is also on the left, with the power turned down a bit. To keep the shadows from being too dark on the right side of the food, place a large piece of white foam core standing to the right of the food (see page 94).

(3) If you don't have Spiderlites or strobes, you can use window light behind your food, and a white reflector in front and on the side.

(4) To get that really shallow depth of field, you need to use the lowest number f-stop your lens will allow (like f/4 or even lower, if your lens can go lower).

(5) This is essentially a product shot, so ideally you'd shoot this using a tripod.

The Recipe for Getting This Type of Shot

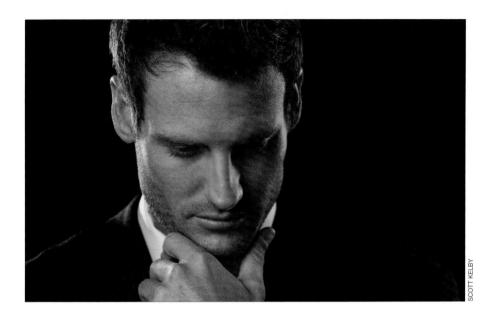

SCOTT KELBY

Characteristics of this type of shot: Hard, chiseled light on both sides of your subject's face, and a dark, dramatic, sharp look to the final image.

(1) This popular look takes three lights. You need two lights placed behind and on either side of your subject, aiming diagonally in at the sides of your subject's face.
(2) These two lights need to have a hard edge to them, so you're not going to use a softbox—just the standard metal reflectors and a bare flash bulb on each. To keep the light from spilling everywhere, use a 20° grid spot over each of the reflectors. They do a great job of aiming a beam of light right where you want it.
(3) To keep the light from these two back lights from creating lens flare (and washing out the photo), put a black flag (usually a 24x36" felt rectangle) in front of each light to block the light from entering your camera.
(4) The front light will be a large softbox, to the front and left side of your subject (from our view), which will be powered way down—just enough to add some fill light in his face. He's shot on a black seamless background. Shoot at f/8 to keep everything sharp and in focus, and use a long 200mm lens for a more pleasing look.

The Recipe for Getting This Type of Shot

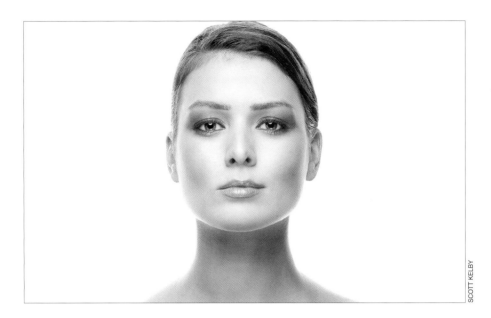

SCOTT KELBY

Characteristics of this type of shot: A clean, bright beauty shot with a wrapping light highlighting the side of your subject's face.

(1) Although you see light wrapping around the sides of her face from both sides, there are only two lights used for this look (which I think makes it even cooler). She is not standing in front of a white background, she's actually standing in front of a large softbox that's about one foot behind her, aiming upward at a 45° angle (just to help keep the flash from creating lens flare, since it would be aiming straight at the camera). So, what you're seeing is the light from that large softbox lighting both sides of her face, the underside of her chin, and the edge of her neck. (See page 50 for the setup shot for this shoot.)

(2) You put the second light, a beauty dish, directly in front of her, but up only about one foot above her head, aiming down at her at a 45° angle (it's almost right in her face—just outside the top of your frame). That lights the front of her face (you can keep the power down pretty darn low, like ¼-power or less).

(3) To keep from having lots of shadows under her eyes, put a large white reflector at her chest level, tilted up just a little bit toward her face. Put it up so high that it's almost in the frame, but not quite. This will reflect light from the beauty dish back onto her face to eliminate shadows and make her eyes nice and bright.

Index

Nikon cameras *(continued)*
sensor cleaning feature, 196
Speedlight stand, 26
time-lapse photography with, 175
video capability on, 189
viewfinder door, 115
VR lenses for, 65
zooming the LCD on, 204
NiMH batteries, 14
noise
high ISO shots and, 148
onscreen vs. print, 113
software for reducing, 172, 179

O

Olivella, Mike, 157
online photo labs, 178
orange gel, 23
outdoor photography, 101–125
arriving early for, 122
backlighting effect in, 121
bright spots avoided in, 107
clouds included in, 109
covering the viewfinder for, 115
deleting bad shots during, 125
framing shots in, 112
graduated neural density filter for, 116
HDR images from, 117–118
hiding modern-day objects in, 107
ISO setting for, 113
lens selection for, 120
light as the subject in, 106
lower-level perspective for, 116
movement effect and, 103
overpowering the sun in, 17
packing list for, 102, 182
panoramas made from, 123
portraits and, 17, 135, 136, 220
postcard images and, 114
puddle reflections in, 112
scouting locations for, 119
shadows included in, 109
star filter effect in, 104
texture shots in, 114

three keys to, 108
underwater shots in, 110–111
vibrant color settings for, 124
white balance and, 105
See also **landscape photography**
overexposing portraits, 140
overpowering the sun, 17

P

packing lists
importance of using, 102
landscape photography, 182
location portrait photography, 184
sports photography, 183
travel photography, 185
wedding photography, 186
panning
freezing motion by, 154, 215
and shooting video, 189
panoramas, 123
people
baby and child photos, 141–143
high vantage point shots of, 130
model releases for, 138
props for shooting, 128, 143
seating for comfort, 129
street shots of, 137
See also **portraits**
percentage of great shots, 188
perspective
child-level, 143
high vantage point, 130
lower-level, 116, 157, 225
Peterson, Moose, 115
photo labs, 178
Photomatix Pro, 118
photos. *See* **digital photos**
Photoshop
Auto Levels adjustment, 111
Auto-Align Layers feature, 219
combining images in, 173, 176
faking reflections in, 84
finding dust spots in, 210
gray card color correction in, 51

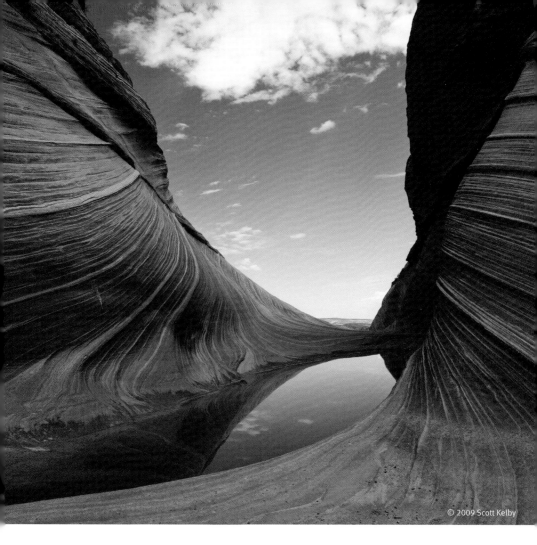

© 2009 Scott Kelby

Color Control Revolutionized

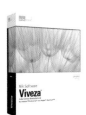

Viveza offers the unprecedented ability to select precise areas of an image and adjust color and light without complicated selections or layer masks.

No other tool does a better job of controlling color and light naturally in your images. Spend more time behind the camera and less time at the computer.

Viveza is available for Photoshop®, Photoshop® Elements, Lightroom®, and Aperture™

"I find myself using Viveza more and more because I just want to get the job done as easy and as fast as possible."

– Scott Kelby
  *President, National Assn. of
  Photoshop Professionals*

Watch the video and try Viveza for free
at **www.niksoftware.com/dpvol3**

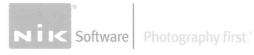

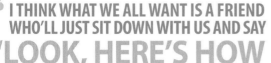
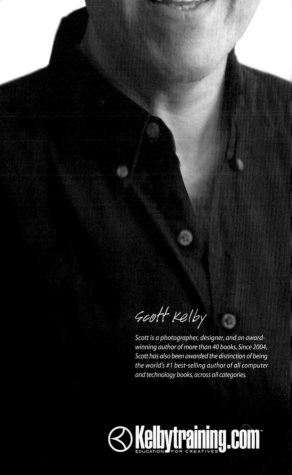

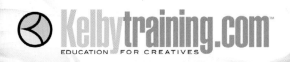
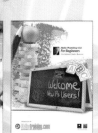 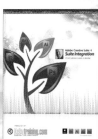 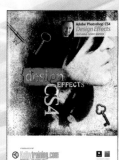 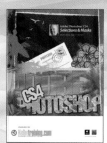 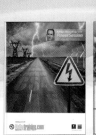
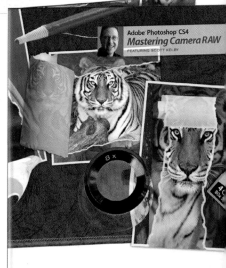
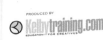

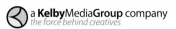

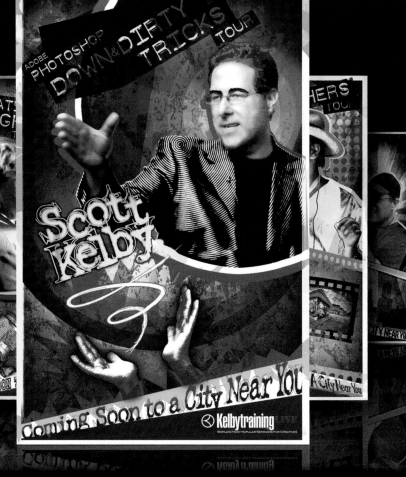

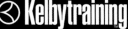

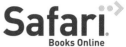
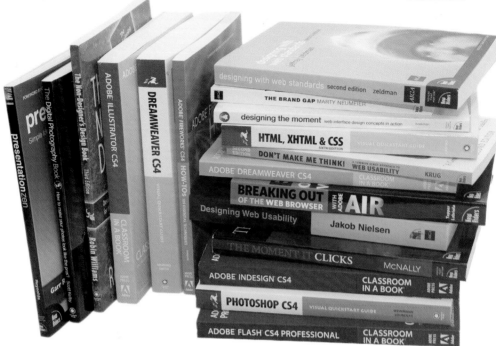